T0090830

Praise for *The Mercy Papers*

"Full disclosure: I may have a little crush on Romm. Not because she's a good writer, although her prose . . . is so fresh and uncompromising it can feel practically impertinent. Nor because of her wit, although she can be startlingly funny . . . Not even because of her fearless, scathing honesty, like a gauntlet thrown down on page after page. It's ultimately her anger that is so magnetic. . . . In Romm's hands, anger becomes an instrument for pursuing truth, an extremely effective crowbar with which to pry back nicety and expose 'something unfettered, something darker.' Often, it's from this unfettered darkness that the author delivers her best lines."

—Leah Hager Cohen, *The New York Times Book Review*

"This powerful book becomes the lifeboat carrying this daughter beyond her mother's death. Her quirky, bold writer's voice grows strong and confident at the bedside and transforms a life cut short into something enduring."

—*San Francisco Chronicle*

"Some people face great sorrow with saintly acceptance. Robin Romm is too human for that, and frank about admitting it. Her willingness to expose herself is brave and may bring solace to others too savaged by grief to let a loved one 'go gentle into that good night.'"

—*Hartford Courant*

"This painful and powerful account manages to offer empathy to anyone whose life has been shaped by grief without condescending to easy consolation."

—*Time Out New York*

"'Rage, rage against the dying of the light,' wrote Dylan Thomas—and that's what Romm does in this searing memoir of her mother's last weeks . . . writing is her transcendence."

—*People*

"There are countless memoirs about death and overcoming grief, but Romm's sheer firepower sets hers apart, capturing all the raw messiness behind her agony."

—*Entertainment Weekly*

"A heartbreaking memoir of staggering genius."

—*Louisville Courier-Journal*

"[*The Mercy Papers*] offers something different, something much truer, about love, loss, and life-changing grief."

—*The Oregonian*

"*The Mercy Papers* is an important work in a young voice."

—*The Plain Dealer*

"It's with this clear-eyed ferocity that Romm faces her mother's death, and while it doesn't make it any easier when it comes—what could?—it does make her memoir such a sharp, striking work that it cheapens it to try to say whether it's good, or whether it might give solace to a grieving reader. It is feverish with loss, gorgeously written."

—*Eugene Weekly*

"Written in the moment and not originally intended for publication, the prose has an immediacy often missing from books that focus on the aftermath and healing. . . . Romm gives voice to the unprecedented grief lying between the realization that death is imminent and the loss itself."

—*Library Journal*

Also by Robin Romm

The Mother Garden

The Mercy Papers

♦ ♦ ♦

A Memoir of Three Weeks

Robin Romm

SCRIBNER

New York   London   Toronto   Sydney

SCRIBNER
A Division of Simon & Schuster, Inc.
1230 Avenue of the Americas
New York, NY 10020

First Scribner trade paperback edition January 2010

SCRIBNER and design are registered trademarks of The Gale Group, Inc.,
used under license by Simon & Schuster, Inc., the publisher of this work.

For information about special discounts for bulk purchases,
please contact Simon & Schuster Special Sales: 1-866-506-1949 or
business@simonandschuster.com.

The Simon & Schuster Speakers Bureau can bring authors
to your live event. For more information or to book an event,
contact the Simon & Schuster Speakers Bureau at
1-866-248-3049 or visit our website at www.simonspeakers.com.

DESIGNED BY ERICH HOBBING

Text set in Granjon

Manufactured in the United States of America

1   3   5   7   9   10   8   6   4   2

The Library of Congress has catalogued the hardcover edition as follows:

Romm, Robin.
The mercy papers : a memoir of three weeks / Robin Romm.
p.   cm.
1. Romm, Robin. 2. Children of cancer patients—Biography. 3. Hospice care.
I. Title.
RC265.6.R66 2009
362.196'9940092—dc22   2008010601
[B]

ISBN 978-1-4165-6788-2
ISBN 978-1-4165-6792-9 (pbk)
ISBN 978-1-4165-6799-8 (ebook)

Some names and characteristics have been changed.

[He] once said to me, "Our lives are just a splash of water on a stone. Nothing more." Then I am the stone on which they fell. And they have marked me.

—NAOMI WALLACE

Part One

♦ ♦ ♦

Barb, our hospice nurse, has bluish teeth and frizzy black hair styled to look like a hunting cap. The skin around her eyes droops and when you talk to her, she takes too long to respond. She wears loose cotton blouses with patterns of clocks or vines. The woman needs to be startled. In one of the many fantasies I've concocted over the last few weeks here, I own a mess of owls and they wait, talons clutching the branch in their ornate cage. When Barb comes—when she looks past me to my mother, past my mother to that voice she listens to when she's not listening to any of us—I will set them free in her face.

Barb comes every few days to clip my mother's socks so her swollen feet will fit or to administer more morphine, more Percocet, more fentanyl. She's building a boat to sail my mother out. She has no interest in my mother's life, the thoughts she had, the cases she won, her family. Barb will build the boat of morphine and pillows and then I will have no mother and the days will be wordless and empty.

I sit on the bed in my childhood room, my cattle dog, Mercy, beside me, and wait for Barb to leave. Sun beats through the small window and skylights, warming the dog's fur. I hold on to my toes. I'd like to ask Barb if she likes her line of work, if there is a particular thrill in being so close to it: someone else's tragedy—how much she gets paid and if she thinks work like this will get her into heaven faster.

Barb must be single. I imagine that she goes home at night, takes off her blouse, unhooks her flesh-colored bra, unbuttons those pleated pants, and slides off her mushy sandals. Maybe she turns on one of her tribal CDs, the sound of drumming thrumming through her condo. Maybe she dances a hesitant little hand dance as she runs water in the tub, leaning into the bathroom mirror to inspect her eyebrows. Some nights she thaws chicken from the freezer and stir-fries it with frozen string beans and crinkle-cut carrots. Some nights it's just cottage cheese and a glass of wine, her feet aching, the television filling her apartment with blues and grays and noise, keeping out the singing of the ghosts of all the people she's sailed.

I can't help thinking that when Barb dies, she'll have to have a hospice nurse. Or maybe she'll get hit by a car and not need one. But if she has a hospice nurse, I wonder what she'll think. I wonder if she'll comply with the way that nurse builds the boat or if she's gotten used to a boat of her own making. I wonder if, in the end, there will be a duel between Barb and her hospice nurse, each struggling over planks and nails. Each trying to get to heaven faster.

"It needs to be where you can always find it," Barb says. In the kitchen, I find my father rummaging in a drawer for some tape. He paws through a tray of pens and, finding the last dregs of a roll, secures the paper crookedly to the fridge. DO NOT RESUSCITATE, it commands. My mother sits rigidly at the table. Just a couple of days ago, with a weak chin and shaking hands, she signed her name.

Barb organizes her secret file. She looks at me, squinting a bit, as if she wishes she could shrink me down into a little figurine. She seems to understand that I will complicate the boatbuilding. *You,* she seems to say, *look like trouble.*

She gets up from the table. "'Bye, Jackie," she says to my mother. She doesn't bother with me. My father walks her out.

Once she's safely down the hill and out of sight, we take our drinks to the deck, presumably to enjoy the sun. One of Barb's hobbies is to mess with my mom's meds, upping the doses until her jaw hangs slack and her gaze turns watery. But today Mom looks lucid. The afternoon light bleaches her skin, revealing the spattering of freckles across her nose and cheeks. Beside her, in old wooden planter boxes, are the remains of the summer flowers. They're starting to turn gray, though the ferns among them are still vivid—green as a child's idea of a crocodile, green as a crayon. The glass table has accumulated a thin film of algae from the wet Oregon winters. Everything here turns green eventually: moss on the roof, the pavement of the overgrown dog run, the trunks of towering fir trees. My mother can't have coffee anymore because of the meds, and besides, her hands have started jerking (a new development—something to do with lack of oxygen). So my dad's given her a big plastic glass of water which she asks me to set on the ground.

"The problem is, Jackie, that if the oxygen tubes come out, and you can't get them back in by yourself, you'll suffocate," my father explains, working the rubbery grip of the wheelchair handle around and around.

My mother trains her eyes on the planter boxes. She seems to be willing the flowers to do something—jump or die, I can't tell which.

She fell again—in the night when no one was with her. My dad and I both heard it: the thud. We ran from our respective bedrooms to find her dazed and annoyed on the navy rug, staring into the woven patterns of men with donkeys and carts like *they* caused her fall.

Falling is hardly the problem, and we all know it. Maybe the problem is God, the lack of God, the lack of mercy, of grace. She's been sick nine years, since she was forty-six. So she takes all these pills and weaves around the house alone. She's attached to tubes to help her breathe. She used to come home from work and run the dishwasher, slap chicken in apricot sauce, gripe about my father's bad habit of leaving plum pits in glasses along the sofa's back, provide our dogs with bones and bowls of mushy food. She'd prowl around after midnight, the late news droning, organizing stacks of bills and baskets of keys into some mom-system my dad and I inevitably messed up. She knew who to call if the roof sprang a leak, if the washer broke, if the little knob inside the fridge fell off. She hired friends of clients to help her move furniture or boxes. She made things happen. Now she's been told she really shouldn't go from the bedroom to the kitchen without the wheelchair and a chaperone.

We keep trying to talk about the problems, but we don't know how. The minute we bring one up, it metastasizes. Maybe the problem is that we keep looking for a problem, something to fix or, at the very least, blame.

"I think we need a night nurse," I say, because it's concrete, a tiny dam to control one part of this flooding. And because the two weeks I've been here have proved we really need one.

My mother turns her scowl on me.

"Where's Lily?" she asks. Lily, my mother's new kitten, has eyes the same color as the table's algae—and they're huge, as if they belong on a much larger animal.

"I don't know, inside somewhere." The other cat, the old cat, Arthur, lies near us on the deck, next to my parents' two vizslas on their ropes. Before the latest downturn, my mother worried over Arthur's declining health. He's lost about half his weight. You can feel the bones beneath his fluffy white fur. Recently he suffered a seizure and my mom sat him under his favorite lamp, nursing him back to health with soft food and soothing words. But right now, no one has energy to worry about the cat—the funny way he jerks his head.

"I think we should bring Lily out here with us."

My mother keeps doing this. She must have a glass of tea right as I'm leaving the house to walk Mercy. She must have a particular cup that no one can find, a brand of chocolate that I have to drive all the way across town to buy. It's a way of rebelling against the wheelchair, a way of continuing to feel effective. I know this. But I'm tired of running pointless errands.

"I don't think Lily wants to come out," I say. "Why don't you pet Arthur?"

"Of course Lily wants to come out," my mother says. She widens her nostrils, sets her jaw.

Before she got sick, my mother won arguments for a living. A trial attorney with a penchant for sleuthing, she found kidnapped children in foreign countries and brought the dirty men to justice; she secured back pay for harassed women, helped disabled sports stars play in the big leagues. My mother believes in yes and no, good and bad, right and wrong, justice and injustice. Unless my conviction matches hers, I won't get anywhere.

I walk stiffly to the sliding doors and shove them open. Arthur follows me into the house, his back leg collapsing in as he lurches forward. Lily lounges on the sofa, licking her leg. She glances up at me, blinks, and begins her rattling purr. Outside, I plunk her on my mother's lap. Her gray bathrobe creates a little nest. She scratches Lily's ears and the kitten drools.

"Why does she do that?" my mother asks quietly. Lily flings her head up toward the sound of my mom's voice and a little fleck of cat saliva sails into the air.

"What do you think about a night nurse?" my dad asks. He's behind my mother. For a moment, he stops messing with the handle grip. He looks terrified. He's looked this way for a year—his sideburns totally white, the skin around his eyes so soft that his eyeballs look like they might fall out.

Lily jumps onto the porch. I grab her and she

gyrates in my hands, flipping her bottom half round and round like a propeller.

"Put her down!" my mother yells, shooting forward in the wheelchair. I drop the kitten. The kitten and I stand there, pressing paws and feet into the wood. "Stop trying to control the cat! You try to control everybody! Why are you so controlling?" Her arms and neck are dotted with red, her hair matted to one side. It looks like we've all been caught in a sudden windstorm, blown sideways for a moment, then frozen.

I feel an ache slowly bloom inside my chest. When it hits my throat, I start to cry. I can't stand the way she's glaring at me—as if *I'm* causing this decline. And so I spin around and run into the house, up the stairs to my bedroom in the loft. Mercy's lost in her ray of sunlight. She perks up when she sees me and thumps her tail on the comforter.

No one comes up to the loft except me—no one ever has—so it hasn't changed much in the ten years I've been gone. Green thumbtacks secure to the wall a Thai shadow puppet of a naked man made out of goat hide. A framed Lichtenstein poster—a relic from my parents' first house, in Nashville—leans against a bookshelf. In high school I wove a peacock feather through the latch in the skylight. It's ratty looking now, covered in dust. Pine needles sit trapped between the screen and the glass.

There's a knock on the door. For a moment, I think it might be my mother. And this thought makes me absurdly happy—if she can get up those stairs, she's not really as sick as she pretends to be and the secret will be exposed. Because I've always felt that somewhere in that failing, graying mother the healthy mom waits, the mom of my childhood who sang show tunes with too much earnestness, who dashed around to meetings in tailored skirts with matching blazers, who bought me body glitter and maroon tights and then shook her head when I wore them. If she could just force through this façade of illness she would emerge vibrant. She would realize that she could put on her nice checkered blouse, her jeans, and soft shoes, and walk with me downtown, past potted plants and children eating ice cream. The world, dumped over on its side, would assume its old shape, would restore itself to the world I knew before this, the world meant for my family.

But it's my father. His hair sticks up in front, accentuating the lack of hair behind it. His stubble looks transparent, like slender pieces of plastic growing from his chin.

"Robin," he says. He's not used to playing the go-between. That has always been my mother's job. "You need to go downstairs."

"No," I say, even though I know I'll go. "I'm not here to get yelled at." Mercy, sensing tension, gets out of the bed and disappears beneath it.

"I know," he says, slumping against the banister outside the room. "Just go downstairs and talk to her."

My mother is parked by the fireplace. She crosses her arms and clamps them to her abdomen. When pissed, she used to storm out of rooms, fling herself around corners, slam stacks of paper against the battered kitchen tile. You never saw her face, just her compact form disappearing, reappearing. Now I see the minutiae of rage—the way her lashes quiver as her eyelids spasm. The way she grinds her teeth.

"I'm sorry," my mother says. She doesn't look sorry, she looks like she's just seen a tiny explosion out of the corner of her eye. "We don't have time for this."

This only makes me angrier—that we've all been placed at the mercy of her disease, that it's trapped us in this house, warping even our arguments. It's not an apology she's giving me, it's a reminder of the time constraint.

"Fine," I say, pinching the skin on my arm. I can't look at her. I wish I were back in Berkeley. I wish I were somebody else—one of my fresh-cheeked friends in graduate school who for the last nine years took time for granted. Someone who didn't have to think about each day, whose cup of coffee on the deck in the morning didn't feel so fucking temporal.

The kitten struts by us on her way to the litter box. My mother and I both stare. Lily feels it. She turns to look at us. She seems to be thinking something; there's a spark in her eyes. Maybe she's contemplating her power, her role as peace provider, distracter, dispenser of balm. I try to imagine what it would be like to be this kitten, to be helpless and innocent, to walk to the litter box completely in the moment. To feel warm and full and settled. To be loved in a simple, untarnished way. Lily narrows her eyes. Then, with her back to us, she squats and pees on the hardwood floor.

♦ ♦ ♦

My mother got diagnosed the summer after my freshman year of college. My best friend, Camas, and I had recently moved to different states. We wanted to be together and we wanted to be poets, so we reunited that summer back in Oregon. When I first met Camas, sophomore year of high school, she wore long skirts in earth tones, baggy cotton leggings, and pretty silver earrings with little beads dangling down. In the first memory I have of us together, we are walking down High Street toward the converted chicken factory, which served as a covered market and food court, toting our satchels empty of books, cutting a class to go eat hash browns—a signature vice of mine. She was shy but intuitive, smarter than most of my other friends, interested in books and painting and scrawny boys who played music. A week or so later, I invited her to spend the night. For hours, we played guitar and burned incense and tried on thrift-store dresses I'd collected— paisley tunics, gauzy rhinestone numbers, or my favorite lime green 1920s shift with yellowing lace that I wore all the time over fraying jeans. Then, when night came, we put on trippy instrumental music and started talking. We dreamed about what our lives would mean, what kind of books we would write, whether or not art was life and what it felt like to be a tree. So often, when we were together, we lost track of time, talking and talking until our throats hurt. Together, it always felt we were on to something, some pulse that would carry us through life, making our existence more interesting than that of the beer-drinking, pot-smoking kids we went to school with. And that night, Camas looked out the bedroom window and saw a small light in the sky. A UFO! A secret message! We stayed up all night trying to figure out what it meant.

Camas went to Ohio for college and I went to Rhode Island and we wrote long letters to each other on old magazines or on weird Xeroxes we'd find in Kinko's. I still have the ones she wrote, stored in envelopes made out of photographs, out of glitter and leaves. We missed each other, so we moved to the Oregon coast to follow our dream of being girl Kerouacs. I wrote elaborate nature poetry on cut-up paper bags in the mornings, washing fish guts off trays on the docks all afternoon, growing more and more disillusioned with the girl Kerouac thing. Camas worked an internship at a battered women's shelter. The silver bullet trailer on loan from a friend's family still had its original 1950s trailer furniture, which included a terrible mattress, half rotted out and filled with black specks. We stuck it in the back of the big Ford I was driving and rode around with it for a month, sleeping on a box spring, coils jabbing into our hips, until my mother was diagnosed with cancer and we returned to Eugene.

My memories of the first months of the disease are gone. Through a haze I see the cream-colored wall phone in the kitchen, hear my father's voice yelling at me (he'd been vacationing in Spain with my mother and stayed to hike when my mom found the lump, thinking it was only a cyst). I can remember the texture of a journal with pink pages, the first thing I ran to when my mother said the word. I even remember what emerged that day, through the pen. A kind of begging with music to it. A feeling that I could change the story if I could get it on paper quickly enough.

Unhappy with the treatment in Eugene (the doctors had given a bleak prognosis, then messed up her radiation), my mother finagled a way to see a famous doctor at Memorial Sloan-Kettering Cancer Center in New York. A few times a year, she'd pack her bags and return to her native city: the narrow streets she walked down when she first met my father, the cramped Chinese restaurants that served cheap chow fun late at night. But the New York she visited after the diagnosis was different; instead of family and food, the trips featured a long wait in a sterile lounge. On modern end tables, waxy philodendrons sat next to Kleenex boxes. Stern-looking women doled out wait times from a giant laminate office station in the corner. I often took the train from Providence to stare with my mother at the women without hair—some old and regal in white gauzy outfits, some very young, crammed into tight jeans. After an hour or two, my mother and I would both exit the shells of our bodies. And though it took hours of waiting past our scheduled appointment, my mother never complained. She believed in this place. This doctor promised her ten years when the doctor in Oregon promised her one. If it took four weeks of sitting in the creamy room, listening to the flat voices of other women talk about antidepressants and bodywork against a sound track of classical music, she would do it without question.

Sometimes my father came with her, but in my memory it was just my mom and me in that lounge, awaiting what we silently hoped was a miracle, a new drug, a new test result, a new lymph system, new cells. After the upbeat meetings, which never lasted more than ten minutes (the elfin doctor in his clean spectacles telling her a new treatment had just been developed! Telling her to sign up for a clinical trial! Telling her to take Zoloft and lose weight so she could enjoy all these years he planned to give her!), my mother would take me out to the avenues. Once we squandered some cash on rhinestone eyeglasses. Once we ate dry black-and-white cookies in a fancy bakery. Once she grabbed my arm and ushered me into a small, crowded room full of women at little white tables, their hands under small whirring boxes.

At this point, I had graduated out of the 1920s shift into hand-knitted sweaters and wool army pants. No one in college had ever mentioned manicures; I'd never had one, never seen a manicure parlor. I lived in a communal house with fifteen other kids. We made our soup in pots the size of car engines, left messages for one another in an antique wooden Coke pallet, swapped clothes from a giant cardboard box in the water-bed room.

"Choose a color," my mother said, touching the little black tops of the bottles.

My mother chose a ruby red for her toes and a dark magenta for her fingers. I watched a young woman my age get her nails painted so that they looked clean. I want that, I said. The manicurist carefully coated the base in pink, then with a steady hand, gave me perfect white sliver moons on every finger.

I never talked about the doctor visits with friends. I

said I went to New York, I said it took all day. But I didn't describe the tightening of my rib cage every time I saw a woman walking with Kleenex balled in her fist. I didn't discuss the way it felt to see my mother unbutton her blouse, revealing a mass of purple scarring, a doughy body puffed from drugs. I showed them my nails, my new glasses, and they felt a little jealous of all my time in the city.

"My mom never takes me shopping," they'd say.

After college, Camas moved to Brooklyn with her new boyfriend. When I came to New York to visit Sloan-Kettering, I sometimes stayed on her futon, needing time away from the cancer. One night her brother was having a party. It had been an awful day in the hospital and I could barely move my legs.

"You should come," Camas said.

I wanted to go, but I couldn't face it. All the people with their plastic cups, talking about internships and art installations as if so much depended on them, on their opinions, on their ideas about Brecht and sexual diversity. I couldn't be around so many healthy people in their twenties, their eyes lit up with the frenzy of being young and lucky.

"I can't go," I said.

"You should really come," Camas said. She, too, had graduated out of vintage dresses and long skirts and into fitted sweaters, still in earthy tones.

"I'm too tired," I said.

The next night, I accompanied her to a bar in Harlem. We met her brother there and drank whiskey in the thick smoke. After two drinks, Camas shoved the table and accused me of being a shitty friend. I felt I was better than everyone, she said. I didn't want to experience her life, talk to her boyfriend. I wanted to come to New York and be the center of attention, stay on her sofa and ignore the changes going on with her. I stared at her, stunned into calmness, tracing the rim of my whiskey glass with my thumb. My quiet further upset her and she ran out of the bar. In the subway tunnel, we sat awkwardly, waiting for a delayed train, pretending to work through whatever it was we were in. But I can still feel the feeling I felt that night—as though I had shrunken down to miniature and was being pulled further and further away from my life. I could move my arms, try to swim back to the world I'd entered a few years ago—the world of my twenties—but the motion got me nowhere. It simply exhausted me. I left the next day confused, remote, unable to explain myself.

♦ ♦ ♦

About two and a half weeks ago, Suzanne called. "Robin, you have to come home. Your mother's fingers are blue."

I'd finally returned to Berkeley after a summer spent in Eugene, ostensibly to be with my mother for the end that didn't come. I stood, phone crammed in between shoulder and neck, folding clothes. "What do you mean her fingers are blue?"

Martha and Suzanne, my mother's law partners, had talked to a client who worked as a nurse. When the patient's fingers turn blue, Suzanne said, there are no more than four days left. "You need to come."

My boyfriend, Don, perched on the side of my bed as I packed a bag for four days. A green thermal shirt, two green T-shirts, a green sweater, and three pairs of jeans.

"Should I bring clothes for a funeral?" I asked him, staring at the closet.

"What?" he said. I fingered an old black skirt. I looked at him, his long fingers toying with themselves, his eyes wide and face blank. He looked like a child, like someone requiring a hug. I turned away.

"I don't know," he said. He stood and placed himself between me and the bag, holding his arms out as if he were available in case I wanted to faint gracefully into an embrace. I had no intention of fainting gracefully into an embrace. The idea of collapse in any form irritated me, as did the tears welling up in his eyes, shiny and helpless. I yanked the black skirt off the hanger. Then I let him hold me while he cried. But the only thing in my mind was when we should pick up my new dog, Mercy, who was being spayed at the vet's, and where we could stop for gas on the way to the freeway, how we could make the drive in the least amount of time. I would pack food. I would fill water bottles. I threw the black skirt to the back of the closet.

The next morning, we picked up the dog. "You'll have to take out those staples in a week," the vet told us. I looked at Mercy's shaved belly, the dark marks that held sides of her together. The vet must have noticed my hesitation because he warned me that if I didn't get them taken out, they'd be covered by her skin, stuck inside of her permanently. We loaded her into the back-seat and headed north.

As we summited the Siskiyou Pass, I felt something soar by, just out of reach, like a bird or a ghost.

"What if we're too late?" I asked Don. I dug my fingers into the stitching of my car's seat. He pressed his foot harder on the gas. The mountains loomed on either side of us, dark trees, vistas.

"No, we'll make it," he said, but his arms were stiff on the wheel. The lines on his brow grew deep and dark. "Give them a call." My reception was out. Pricks of heat bounced up my neck. The dog woke up and began to lick her stitches, whining.

"I can't call," I said. "It doesn't make any difference. We can't get there any faster." And I cried looking out at the craggy rocks in shades of orange and gray, the gashes of rivers, a vulture swooping by.

Six hours later, we pulled into the cul-de-sac. My stomach hurt. I dashed up the steps, careful to avoid skidding on the algae, imagining that when I flung open the red door, I would find silence, men with a gurney, my father sitting at the kitchen table over a glass of Scotch, his palms covering his eyes. But the house was full of women. "Robin!" Martha cried from the big orange sofa. "Hi hi hi! You got here!" The silver and bronze sculpture of mountains and trees hung boldly on the wood above the fireplace, catching circles of lamplight. My mother held Lily under a thick cro-cheted afghan. I went over to pet the kitten. My mother's fingers looked fine.

"You two must be hungry," Martha said, jumping up and clasping her hands together. She wore a short work skirt and transparent hose. The muscles of her long legs twitched. "What do you want to eat?"

Suzanne sat on the bench under the sculpture. She put her elbows on her knees and pressed the back of her neck. Her reddish hair looked dark and flat in the dim lamplight, like a slab of burlap. Martha shot her a look. Suz sat up straight, smoothed her slacks with her palms. "You want some food?" she asked.

"What are you doing here?" my mother asked when the rest of them went to the kitchen. "You have school."

I met her eyes, which were unusually cold, as if challenging me to admit that I'd bought into the idea she would die, just like everyone else.

Tonight, Martha and Suzanne, have driven up to have dinner. My mom's too tired from Barb and the afternoon fight with me to join us. My father bends over his plate, both elbows on the place mat, legs crossed so that his knee pokes over the table's edge. His prize vizsla, Sol, rests his head on my father's leg, staring at him lustily. My father is the only person I know who doesn't fidget under the weight of another's stare. For almost a minute I've been testing him, but he continues to eat his salmon, unfazed. He watches the center of the plate, or rather looks right through it to some other dimension where he prefers to exist.

Mercy comes tearing downstairs. A huge roar erupts as Sol sees her. He puts a red paw on her back and tries to fit his mouth over her nose. "STOP," I roar

20

back at him and he looks at me sideways, prideful. But he stops. Mercy waggles over, collapsing next to my chair.

"What about a South of the Border," Suzanne says. "Like border collie. South of the Border . . . Collie! Or how about something with sour mix in it."

Martha has her hands folded under her chin. She's thinking.

"A Whisker Sour," I say, momentarily breaking my gaze at my father to look at Suz. She's sprawled over one of the wooden chairs, long-limbed, a smear of grease evident on the thigh of her brown slacks.

"Yeah!" Martha says. She scrunches her face. "Oh, that's a good one!" My father manipulates a chunk of salmon off its silver skin, dragging it across the plate before getting it to balance on his fork. It's a large piece of fish, the pinkness darkening as the candles flicker.

There's nothing to do while my mother sleeps. I'm too anxious to get any real work done—I've dropped out of my graduate program to be here—and I haven't been able to write fiction. I can't imagine beyond this house, beyond what's impending. It's all too urgent. So I've announced that I am going to write a doggie cocktail book with a drink for every breed. *Hair of the Dog,* I'm calling it. Martha, Suzanne, and I have become a bit addicted to the project. My mother attempted to join in a few times, but she can't think fast enough anymore.

"What do we have so far?" Suzanne says, leaning over me to see the list we've compiled: Jack Spaniel, Silky Perrier, The Chi-Chi Chow Chow, Pekinese Freeze.

"Lassie," Martha says. "Lassie Come Home, no. Lassie on Ice. What alcohol starts with *L*? Lemon something? Limone. The Lazy Lassie. Lucky Lassie. Lacerating Lassie."

"Yikes, Marth." Suzanne pulls her chin to her neck to giggle.

"Sassy Lassie!" Martha says. "Sassy Lassie." She leans over to watch me write it down.

"Your handwriting is just like your mom's," Suz says.

Suzanne and Martha shared a law practice with my mother for nearly ten years. Bright paintings covered the walls: nests of abstract pinks, figurative images of women with baskets in the desert. Masks of Suzanne's face, made out of painted clay, hung boldly over the doors. Geodes, sage bundles, and pieces of blown glass cluttered their bookshelves, distracting visitors from the intimidating tomes behind them. My mom had the first office. The smell of nice things wafted into the waiting area: expensive perfume, leather, wood varnish. Her rosewood desk curved into an L. A leather briefcase leaned beside it, embossed with her initials. On matching bookshelves, photos in thick glass or ceramic frames stood beside puzzles of chickens and dogs. Me on top of windy Mount Shasta with my father, me in a bunny outfit in a photo booth, me in a vintage blazer and John Lennon glasses holding a piece of driftwood. She displayed my early attempts at woodcraft: a propeller plane, a sailboat. Glass paperweights held down pieces of paper. A giant glass diamond, a gift from my father's mother, sat next to a gavel. Draped over her leather chair, a soft black jacket, a handwoven scarf. She worked for years after her diagnosis. She loved her clients, felt protective of her partners. She worried that without her, they'd screw up the books and sink.

Now her office belongs to a man named Charlie. The day they stopped saying her name when they answered the phones, my mother locked herself in the bedroom and cried.

Martha and Suz wear jade good luck charms my mother brought back from New Zealand years ago. They've canceled meetings and postponed cases. "We're *partners,*" Martha will say when anyone remarks on how much time they spend at the house.

After dinner, Suz and I sit, brainstorming breeds while Martha and my dad take in the plates. I can hear the clank of porcelain against steel. One of them starts the dishwasher and the house fills with a methodical swishing.

"Have you gotten out of the house today?" Suzanne asks. "Or did Nurse Ratched kill your momentum?" She's been on me to take my new dog, Mercy, to the park, to join a yoga class, go do some life drawing. When she suggests these things, she looks riddled with guilt, as if she knows before she speaks how pointless her suggestions are.

With the exception of accompanying Mom to the doctor's office, I haven't left the cul-de-sac in days. My father takes Mercy up the mountain every morning with his two big vizslas, eliminating the need for much more than a walk around the yard in the afternoon.

Martha settles herself next to me. Her skin could

belong to someone twenty years younger. Silvery hair and a few smile lines near her eyes provide the only clues to her age.

"You should go to the movies!" Martha says.

Mercy's leaning against me under the table and I scoot my chair back so I can drag her to my lap. She rests her body against my chest—she's the same size as my torso—and her warmth seeps through my T-shirt.

My mother knew in early spring that the cancer had begun its victory lap. When she called to tell me that it spread to her liver, she couldn't even get through the sentence. "I'm so sorry," she kept repeating.

My mother is going to die, I thought, my mind on a loop. *I need a dog. She's going to die. I need a dog.*

"You don't need a dog," my mother said to me. "That's about the last thing you need. You need a dog like I need a hole in the head."

That spring, after spending hours online and in bookstores researching breeds, I began to foster dogs for a rescue group in Berkeley. I had a roommate, Laura, in her third year of architecture school. We'd lived together for years, but these days she rarely came home due to the long hours required by her studio. Laura's ambivalence toward dogs made asking this of her difficult. But she must have seen the need in my gestures, the way I sat hour after hour in front of a screen taking notes on breeds (pugs: funny, bad respiratory systems; pointers: high-strung, athletic). When I finally got the courage, she looked at me dully, held her cup of coffee up, and stared at the pattern on the porcelain. "Sure," she said, glancing at our two cats sleeping on the rug. "If that's what you want, go for it."

Ollie, the first dog I brought home, had black skin around his mouth though the rest of him was chestnut brown. An indeterminable mix of breeds, he resembled a Labrador, but with the bone structure of a papillon. The first thing Ollie did, upon seeing my small dining room, the wool rug covered in cat hair and dust, was get sick in steaming piles. I sighed and surveyed the situation—he shivered and blinked. Fleas fell off when I dragged a nail down his back. He didn't quarrel with me when I placed him in the tub. He submitted easily, tail between his legs. I ran a washcloth over his body until no more dirt came off.

"Oh my God," Don said when he arrived. "You are ridiculous." He sat next to me on the sofa to fondle the dog. I held Ollie like a baby, still swaddled in towels. "He's sick," I said.

Don shook his head at me. "No, you're sick," he said, and then began to scratch Ollie under the chin. The dog slowly closed his eyes.

"Wa-ow," Don said. "So cute." The next morning we put him in the backseat of my car, stopped for coffees, and took him to the dog park. I'd been so sad, so despondent, but that morning we all felt like wagging our tails. The sun shone brightly over the green rolling hills of the park and the air smelled of salt water and mown grass. Ollie threw his head skyward, breathing it all in, wagging his rump and nodding at other dogs. I felt the most normal I'd felt in a month. I felt like a girl in my twenties with her dog and boyfriend and coffee by the glittering bay. We let Ollie off the leash to toss a ball for him. He stayed close to us, fetching when we asked, politely dropping the ball at our feet.

But it was the first dog I'd ever fostered. I wasn't ready to commit. I took Ollie to the adoption fair, where he wagged his tail and tilted his handsome face at the people walking by. A woman with a cape of black hair fell to her knees in front of him. "What a darling!" she breathed. I felt a jealous pang, but I walked away.

I spent the rest of the day crying. Don put his hands on my back and shoulders, but I couldn't feel them. I'd lost Ollie and I would lose my mother, and life only let you see joy so it could steal it away.

Later that day, a friend asked me why I would deny myself the dog. I was about to go home for the summer, I said. I'd rented a studio so I could be with my mom in Oregon and this dog didn't fit in with that plan. "Get the dog. Make it work," she said.

I took the streets with the fewest stop signs, my heart pounding all the way to the adoption fair. "I want to adopt Ollie," I said to the woman with the clipboard. She drew her unruly eyebrows together as she searched her records. "Sorry," she said. "He got snatched up as soon as you brought him. He's gone to a great home." Again tears, right there on the sidewalk. "There are plenty of dogs out there," the woman said. "Seriously, sister, it'll be all right." So I took home a rust-colored Belgian shepherd and named him Lyle. Once I left him outside for an hour and he chewed through the wooden patio table. Another time, I ran out to get something from my car and Lyle, in a desperate attempt to keep our connection, tore through the front blinds with his teeth so he could see me. At the dog park, he didn't stay close; he darted off, collapsing in front of passersby with a flopping pink erection. I felt low those days, like my blood ran thick through its piping, and I hated having to kneel over Lyle with the leash, apologizing as I gestured to his privates. After a month, I looked long and hard at that dog and he looked questioningly back at me. And then, without tears, I loaded him in the car and took him to the adoption fair. Next came an Australian shepherd named Jasper who couldn't sit still, couldn't walk on a leash, couldn't make eye contact. He jumped at the door, gobbled his food, slapped a giant speckled tongue this way and that. He wasn't the one, either. Then I took in two Chihuahua brothers who seemed to have choreographed a routine: They would run and jump onto the dining room chairs, then onto the table. Once there, they would fling themselves toward the wall, dispensing arcs of urine as they jumped.

And after this slew of canines, I went to Oregon, to live in a rented studio. While there, I journeyed to the garages of backyard breeders, looking at pugs, halfway convinced that their snorting and smashy faces would distract me from my mother's mercurial illness (which had stopped progressing briefly due to an experimental drug). But the breeders were all the same: smokers with floral couches and creepy gazes. I just couldn't take home one of their dogs.

When I returned from that visit in August, I felt it was time to put an end to the yearning. Again, I spent hours online, this time looking only at shelters. I wanted to save something. And I'd decided I wanted, needed, an Ollie. Small and sleek, my dog wouldn't need a lot of exercise and could fit in a carry-on bag so that I could fly to Oregon on a moment's notice. And then one morning, I found a jpeg of a small golden dog, like a shrunken fox, in a shelter three hours east. I called and asked the adoption coordinator about him. "Oh, a handsome devil," she said. "Is he friendly?" I asked. "Pretty friendly," she said. "Maybe a little shy." I didn't listen to the hesitation in her voice.

The Merced County Animal Control was worse than I imagined—a series of trailers and cement dog runs filled with the sound of desperate barking. A woman shaped like a sausage waited to drop off a Chihuahua bitch that had become sterile and could no longer breed. The dog shivered on the reception counter as the volunteer processed paperwork.

Sure that the shrunken fox would come home with me, I'd paid for him in advance. But when the adoption coordinator brought him out of the cage, he didn't look at me. He began to sniff the grass, every once in a while glancing up furtively. Instead of animal wisdom, he embodied paranoia. His little black nose worked over the blades, as if he wanted to burrow between them. We waved a plastic duck at him, but he didn't take to it. The bark of a pit bull caged nearby got his attention and he barked back, shrill and obsessive. He barked and barked and barked. The woman waited for me to say something. I must have looked crestfallen under the big elm tree, my hands shoved into my sweatshirt pockets. I'd hung my heart on returning with a dog that day. I'd woken with that particular happiness I could never keep: I'm a girl in her twenties getting a dog! I'd trotted to the car that morning feeling like all my joints had been oiled.

The dog gave a few last barks before starting on the grass routine again. I shook my head, aware of a heaviness seeping back into my bones. "That's not the right dog," I said.

The adoption coordinator squinted at me. Her brown hair looked singed at the tips. She scooped up the shrunken fox. "What are you looking for, hon?" she asked. I told her I wanted an excessively loving and loyal dog. She turned toward the kennels.

Within minutes, a speckled dog with a pea head and barrel chest came squiggling toward me, her entire body electric with joy. She leaped onto me, licked my hands, and dropped to the ground, rolling belly up. I knelt next to her and she looked at me, pointing her narrow nose at my chin. At first she simply looked frantic, but as she calmed under my hand, a dullness flickered in her eyes. It remained only briefly, then disappeared back into the puppy brightness. A kinship so intense and so irrational surged. I named her Mercy, for Merced and for what we all needed then, what we all need right now, here at this table.

"I can't go anywhere without Mercy," I say. The dog presses her black nose into my neck and lifts her paw so it rests on my shoulder.

I don't need to explain to Martha and Suzanne that I've vested Mercy with special powers. Even my mother says that Mercy will have to be the one to carry me past all this. I press my nose into her fur. Her smell—like moss and armpit, mud and river. I could live in it.

"It's criminal that you can't bring her to the movies with you," Suzanne says.

"You should knit a cape," Martha says. "Then you could hide her in it."

"Or a fat suit," says Suz.

"A fat suit," I repeat. Suz starts to giggle again and grabs the stem of her wineglass. She takes a swallow.

"Man, your dad likes nice wine," she says, turning her jaw toward the ceiling. "Gosh, darn."

"Or why not just say she's a guide dog," Martha says, sitting up straight. She's tapping a coaster on the table.

"Yeah! She *is* a guide dog," Suzanne says. "Totally." Suz leans in to scratch Mercy's ears. "Mercy the guide dog's going to get us all out of this pickle." Mercy closes her eyes, and loosens her front legs so that she flops into a heap on my lap. We pet her and pet her, our strokes getting harder and more intense, as if petting Mercy will give us what we need.

"I just can't believe she's thinking about the *movies,*" my father says. It's night now and he can't see me standing in the hallway.

"She wasn't thinking about the movies," Martha says. "She was just talking."

"Her own mother is dying and all she can think about is getting that fucking dog into the movies."

"Richard, it's not like that," Martha says.

30

"Her and her fucking dog."

I walk into his line of vision, and he looks away. Martha shakes her head at me. He inspects the hair on his hands.

My father's father called today to see if we'd like to take him to lunch. He tries to be sneaky when he makes these requests. "Hello," he yelps. He always yelps. "The food here is so terrible! Ham, they're serving. Traif with gravy! What are your plans?" My mother urged us to go out. Her friend Krys was coming up to the house. "We'll be FINE," she said. I think she actually wants us gone. We've been bothering her with our planning, our need to discuss nurses and pills. She hates asking us for help with the wheelchair. She hates the way we mope. She's constantly encouraging my father to hike, go to the store, get out out out out. Maybe she imagines that she can send Krys for bread—that for twenty whole minutes she'd be the boss lady again. She'd sit in the silent house, the high wooden ceiling above her, and tell her big red vizsla Sophie to come to her. She'd stroke Sophie's ears, wheel into the bathroom, stare at herself in the mirror, run her hands through her thin hair, close her eyes. She might fold some laundry or sing off-key, take off her shirt and sit in the sun. For twenty minutes she would be alone, the house all hers, and no hands could touch her.

My father and I don't talk as we peel out of the garage in his slick black car. I turn on the radio and let it talk for us as we make our way across town to where my grandfather lives, in an apartment overlooking a bend in the Willamette River. This part of town used to

31

be grassy and wild when I lived here. Eugene sits in a lush river valley and the town peters out into fields and grassland. But this area has given way to my grandfather's large retirement home and other sterile-looking buildings. Vinyl banners advertising riverfront patios drape across beige and white condominiums. He's waiting for us in the large circular drive. He seems particularly compact, as if trying to cram his entire body into his dirty red Windbreaker. All around him, Canadian geese peck at the grass.

"Howareyou," my grandfather says, curt. I lean in to kiss his cheek and smell a mix of old skin and citrus. His scalp, which I can see if I stand up straight, is as specked as a cardinal's egg.

Before we left, my mother told me about a dream she had the night before. In the dream, men climbed up a pole to protect themselves in gunfights. These dream men would climb and twirl and always land on their feet, firing precisely. My grandfather turned up on the pole, swirling around it, his body like the metal of a fan blade, and he went faster and faster and then let go and landed on his feet. This impressed my mother.

I shove crap off the backseat so I can fasten my seat belt. My father's car always contains unusual refuse. You might find shiny scrolls of paper with the jagged lines of a patient's heart, a coiled and badly beaten stethoscope, sample boxes of medications with names in undecipherable medicalese, mud-encrusted dish towels, a stuffed goose with a hole in its beak—left by Sol.

"I got invited to Andrew's Bar Mitzvah!" my grandfather says.

"Do you want to go?" my father asks, taking a curve very fast. I grab onto the headrest of the seat in front of me. "*Dad.* Jesus." The speed of the car sends my grand-father's head toward the glass of the side window, but he quickly recovers and turns to my father.

"I'm not going!" my grandfather yelps. "How can I go! They know I can't go and they still invite me and then I have to send *money*! They all expect money from me because this child became a teenager or this one got married. And they don't even send thank-you notes!" He shakes his hands in the air; they're speckled, too.

"You're not sending enough money," my dad says, grinning. "There's a minimum. You have to send *enough* money to get the thank-you note."

After we are settled in the covered market, my grandfather sucks on his dentures and chuckles. Since the car ride, he's been thinking. "A minimum!" He repeats this to himself again and again, over his lunch of runny egg salad, punctuating it with a high old-man giggle. "A minimum!"

"We're *FINE*," my mother says when I call. So we decide to capitalize on the time and take in a matinee. My father disappears into the bathroom and I hold out my arm to usher my grandfather down the dark aisle to a seat. I settle in and secretly envy all the people chomp-ing popcorn and candy.

My family doesn't partake in this sort of extrava-gance. Certain aspects of my father's upbringing in Brooklyn housing projects have made their way into our life in Oregon, despite my parents' professional suc-cess. In my life, I have probably ordered a soda at a restaurant four times. I rummage in my purse and find a piece of linty gum. My grandfather looks as though he'd be swallowed alive by the velvet seat if not for the enormous red baseball hat he found in the car. It sits cockeyed on his little bald head.

My grandfather's afraid of my mother. And since she went off treatment, he has not been to see her. He hasn't offered to help, he hasn't sent flowers. My mother says that he has to come up to the house to say good-bye. It's not because she wants to see him, not because she'll miss the way he shuts down any emotional conversation, choosing instead to quote the *Times* at length or yelp about Herzl Street in the Brooklyn of his dreams, but because she knows how bad she looks, that her dark eyes are migrating to the sides of her head from all the narcotics, that her face is perpetually shiny and creased from the mask she uses for oxygen. Her hair falls in greasy clumps, she hunches over and can't breathe. She's a walking confrontation with decline. And she wants to shove this in my grandfather's face. Even as she fades out of this world, she's a trial lawyer, she's obsessed with justice. And he's behaved badly, so he has to pay.

My grandfather sighs, a sigh that says many things. It says: Finally I am in a velvet seat and out of that crazy car with your father who hates me. It says: What movie have you taken me to? It says: Robin, don't ever grow old.

"Dad's having a hard time," I say. "I've been wondering, maybe, if there's something we can do to help him."

My grandfather shrugs hard, like there's water on

his back. I stare at him, willing him, for once, to say something sage.

"I think I know what I'll do," my grandfather finally says. The lights are starting to go down. I glance behind us for my dad. "I'll tell him *my* problems."

"How is that helpful?" I ask.

"It'll take his mind off *his* problems."

"I don't think that sounds like a very good idea," I say.

"But my problems are so small!" my grandfather squeals. "*The New York Times!* I get these bills! They're crazy!" He's quite worked up now, which means he's gone from a squeal to a shriek. "WHAT DO THEY WANT FROM ME?"

I wave at my father scanning for us by the doors.

"I still don't see how that's helpful. You could tell him that you love him."

"Oh, Robin." From his tone, it sounds like I've just spilled wine on a white carpet. "I told him yesterday I was worried about him!" His small eyes shine, his hands shine, spit glitters on his bottom lip. "I *rely* on him!"

It's not the same thing, but I don't have a chance to argue. The previews come on and my father sits beside me, thrusting his long legs out into the aisle.

My grandfather never asks about my mother, though sometimes he corners me to ask, "Robin, how are you helpful?," to which I have no response. My grandmother died three years ago. For months afterward, my grandfather lit into my father every time he saw him.

You killed your mother! he'd scream, his high voice

cracking, tissues wadded in his fists. *She suffered at your hands!*

My father, the doctor, couldn't stanch the bleeding. And she was on hospice but she pleaded with my dad not to let her die like that and the bathroom was covered with blood—so much blood, how could she still be alive? *Don't let me die like this!* And so my father called an ambulance and overrode hospice and they gave her transfusions until she just couldn't take them anymore and she died, terrified and unprepared at eighty-nine. And my grandfather blamed my dad. He didn't like the boat that sailed her out. Not that boat. Not without him in it.

Sometimes now, I will study my grandfather's bent frame, his beaky nose, and try to imagine what he looked like as a young boy, curled in a twin bed, twisted in sheets in a tenement. His face looks so old now that it's impossible to imagine it smooth. The closest I can come is an old sepia-toned photo of my father, his baby mouth revealing bright new teeth, the camera's flash a festive fire in his eyes. I've never seen a photograph of my grandfather as a child, or of his father and mother. If I had photographs, would I be able to unravel the clues? Would I know why he stares off into a dark place when you talk to him? Why he turns off his hearing aid before dinner?

My mother and I often speculate as to why he does these things. In fact, just a few months ago we spent the entire two-hour drive from Yachats to Eugene winding through possible reasons. Is this his way of maintaining power? Is it deep avoidance of intimacy or authenticity?

Is it some bizarre manifestation of insecurity, hard to recognize in someone so old? We never get anywhere and eventually my mother will throw her hands in the air, roll her eyes, and say: "This is such a waste of time! There's no reason; he's just nuts!" But I wonder, was there a distinct moment when he shut down? I think of his refusal to see my mother. Maybe the death of his own mother froze him in his tracks. She was young— younger than my mother is now. His father was a drunk and a gambler and the early 1930s were dark times. Her death sent him flying like a flare into a black sky. Maybe when he felt himself hurled out and fading, he decided that life was this: merely something to survive.

My father fled to Oregon when he became a doctor, convincing my mother to go with him. Unlike my grandfather, who attended shul every week, my father rarely went to temple. Instead he discovered moun-taineering, the mineral smell of rock and snow, the burning of a glacier at sunrise. He strapped himself to ropes and packs and felt far from those cramped tene-ment rooms with radiator heat, with cupboards full of photographs and letters and records and packages of panty hose bought on sale at the drugstore. On a moun-tain, as night becomes dawn, you can see the sun and the moon on either side of you. You can actually see the passage of time.

And while he did this, while he was instructing me as I trudged up mountains after him, to straighten my leg so the blood could rush into my muscles—kick into the snow and lift, straighten, rest—as he was showing me *his* relationship to God, my grandmother stood in the spare room of their apartment and watched the Lincoln Continental they never drove, parked in a numbered lot below their building in Brooklyn. She woke three times a night to make sure it was still there.

Two years before my grandmother died, some distant cousins went to see them in New York. They're old, the cousins said. They can't live like that anymore.

My father refused to hear this. "Well, they can't move here," he declared. He wouldn't discuss it. And so the problem fell to my mother. She said, "You're getting older." She said, "What'll you do if something happens? Who will take care of you?" And my grandparents claimed they had nieces and nephews in Long Island. My grandmother had practically raised her dead sister's son. Surely he would agree to help if no one else would. "Call them all," my mother said, years of lawyering making her voice stern. "See if any of them will commit."

They would not. And so, it was decided.

"You wouldn't believe how terrible it was," my mother said. She was sick then, but she didn't look like she does now. She could still breathe. She wore blush on her cheeks and it sparkled. Her thick crimson shirt matched a pair of soft red sandals and a shiny red pedicure. We sat at the kitchen table. She'd just returned from packing the apartment in Sheepshead Bay. "I don't think those two even like each other. That apartment was toxic. You should have heard the things they said." My mother raised her shoulders, shuddered, and looked away. "I thought maybe if we could get them here your father would finally be able to reconnect with his family." She set her teacup down and looked at me. "But maybe I was wrong."

And they wouldn't throw anything away. My mother packed boxes of toilet paper, bought on sale at Waldbaum's, and paid to have them shipped to Eugene. Now there is a wall of toilet paper in one of my grandfather's bathrooms. Since my grandmother's death, he's moved into a retirement home, but he took the toilet paper with him. The rolls, some of them yellow with age, go all the way to the ceiling.

Since the death of her own mother, my mother's been more interested in Jewish rituals and rights. Though she didn't go to services or keep a kosher kitchen, she helped the rabbi negotiate a better employment contract with the temple's board and now the temple sends people to bring us food. Tonight, a woman named Rena will bring over fish garnished with capers and olives.

Rena hasn't arrived yet, but I think she's the one with glasses and blond hair. She's in her fifties and my ninety-one-year-old grandfather, outside after Yom Kippur services, remarked that she looked just like an eighty-six-year-old woman who moved into his retirement home last week. Rena tried to be good-natured about this. My grandfather looked deranged and gleeful. The spit wad on his lips shone brightly under the streetlamp, the dark splotches on his face suggesting darker things beneath.

My mother is sitting in the den, watching the news, when the doorbell rings. Rena is indeed the blond woman with glasses. Dressed in a sharp black pantsuit and pearls, she struts theatrically into the den, her head held high (so brave!) to say hello to my dying mother. I know it's a nice gesture, this. But she has never come up here before in the nine years of this dying. Are these people trying to bring us shards of grace? Or are they simply gawking?

When she leaves, we serve ourselves from her white baking dish, the handles slightly discolored. The fish has green olives, capers, pimentos, and figs and has been cooked to a sawdusty texture. My father, mother, and I sit at the small round table in the kitchen and push bits of it around and around. My mother makes little piles of capers, little piles of olives. Rena is not as experienced with these matters as we are. What dying woman craves capers?

In the morning I spend an hour in bed, unable to move any of my limbs because there are skylights above me and the rain is the first soothing thing I recognize. In this moment, there's only the dampness in the air from the open windows and the smell of wet wood and cloud. And I want to be only these things: smell and skin.

When I finally get downstairs, my mother sits at the kitchen table, Mercy at her feet. She's trying to puff morphine smoke from the blue nebulizer, but no one has filled it with morphine yet. She jerks it up to her face, misses her mouth, drops her hands to the table, and tries again.

Her fingers are blue at the tips.

"Why are your fingers blue?" I'm almost growling and a heat flashes into my head, making me feel woozy.

Blue fingers—I try to remember exactly what Suz and Martha said. Four days? Starting when? When did this happen?

I must look demented, standing here in my night-shirt, my angry face creased from medicated sleep, my hair ratty, my feet bare. I must look as though I am about to seize her hands and shake them free of that awful color. And she glances down at the little blue contraption, its mouthpiece like that of a flute, puzzled and childlike.

"I ate blueberries," she said.

Hospice has assigned us a bath aid. My mother calls her Brunhilda, though her name is probably Melody or Beth. Brunhilda barks when she speaks. She's built like a bull. Whatever her failings, I'll give her this: She is not trying to get to heaven faster. She seems to have very concrete desires. Today she suggests that we install safety railings in my mother's glass shower.

"I have a beautiful shower!" my mother snaps. "And I'll be damned if I ruin it with that shit."

It's true that my mother has a beautiful bathroom. She redid the floors many years ago in cream ceramic tile. An exposed wood ceiling slopes over a bathtub and on the wall beneath it she hung all the artistic attempts of mine that feature fish: a hammered tin fish I made in elementary school, a fish mosaic (extremely ugly) I made in college. My mother is a Pisces. Her towels are orange and thick. Ceramic mugs glazed in shimmering blue sit next to matching soap dishes and jars.

Brunhilda doesn't like to get wet. She likes dying people who sit nicely in tubs with extendable hoses and hold on to safety railings while she wipes them with liquid antibacterial soap. I imagine her usual clientele are frail women with powder-colored hair, their faces free of blood, their bones nearly weightless. My mother is still very much in her body and no one, not even my dad, would be able to lift her over the lip of the bathtub to sit on the white plastic bench. So Brunhilda has to get in the shower with her and this means she must touch the spray.

Everyone finds this scenario irritating.

On her way out, Brunhilda stops to talk to my father.

"How'd it go today?" he asks. His voice has changed this year. It's as though there are little bullets of lead hanging from his words. He holds a torn envelope and a bill. He appears to be studying them. Brunhilda's face is hidden by very long, thick blond bangs and she wears the rest of her hair in a scalping ponytail.

"It was better," she announced. "But I still got wet because you won't put in an extendable hose."

My father doesn't look up. "Hazards of the job," he says.

My mother's friend Ellen arrives at the house bearing bags of groceries. My grandfather loves Ellen—not for her unfailing friendship to my mother, not for her comic timing or her ability to listen with her whole being, but because her father ran a catering business in Brooklyn. "He catered your Bar Mitzvah!" he shrieks at my dad. "Adler's Catering! I can't believe it! An Adler! All the way out here in Ory-gone!" He cannot get over the fact of this most recent exodus—Jews in the Pacific Northwest. When I began to apply to college, he shook his head at me pityingly. What college would admit a child—a *Jewish girl* child—from the hinterlands of Eugene, Oregon? Ellen sets the bags on the counter and gives me a meaningful hug, leans away, and grips my shoulders. "How are you, sweetie?" she asks. I smile and shrug.

Ellen used to be a chef, a fact I learned only recently in a conversation with my mother. She's been an attorney for as long as I can recall. Tonight she unpacks the snow peas, shrimp, little jars of sauces. She's brought the book she promised to bring—a little paperback full of Chinese recipes.

In February, my mother turned fifty-six. I'd come from Berkeley to celebrate with her. Birthdays, to my mother, always radiated joy. Even before she got sick, she reveled in marking the passage of years, in dreaming up gifts and writing sappy, loving cards that always made me feel both irritable and loved—irritably loved. "Don't buy me anything," she said. "I don't need any more stuff. Just buy something for yourself."

I tried not to pay attention, wandering around the shops in the covered market. I picked up bracelets embedded with amethyst, her birthstone. I ran my hand over expensive hand-carved bowls. She couldn't leave the house. She didn't want cooking gear. I looked at the flowers on display. They'd look pretty for a moment by the sink, but then you'd have to watch them shrivel and die.

The first gift I bought my mother with my own money was a pewter brooch of a storm cloud with tiny lightning bolts hanging from it by metal rings. My mother, in her Ellen Tracy and Liz Claiborne, never would have chosen it, but to me, at the time, it represented a connection to power—something my mother inarguably embodied. She opened the gift and exclaimed over it, kissed my cheek, and wore it pinned to her designer jacket for months, until the lightning bolts fell off. She still has it. The other day, when looking for a ring she thought she lost, I went pawing through the jewelry in her underwear drawer and there it was, gray and chunky, sitting amid much nicer pieces—my grandmother's pearls, a heavy gold chain from my father.

I returned from the stores empty-handed. I liked my mother's birthday. I felt a thrill when I got it right, like the time I gave her the journal I'd made for her, with collaged writing prompts on every page. Or the painted gourd with the African bead handle she kept on her fancy table. I knew she loved presents, loved beauty above most things. But I didn't want to be left with a fancy salad bowl, an amethyst bracelet. After a few hours of this, I drove to the grocery store.

I spent the afternoon making and icing cupcakes. With as steady a wrist as I could muster, I wrote *Happy Birthday Mom,* a pink letter on each little top. I arranged them on a platter and stuck candles around the circumference, hiding the whole thing in the dining room. Later that night, I wheeled her into the kitchen. She sat at the table in her worn nightgown. I dimmed the lights and marched in wielding my creation. I smiled broadly, spoke with targeted perkiness. This was a *birthday,* a *birthday.* When I set the platter down in front of her, I had to blow out the candles because her diaphragm was damaged, paralyzed from crudely performed radiation, and she gripped the armrests of the chair and started to cry.

There's so little we can do, so little that will plug, even for a moment, the hole that bleakness pours through. I have been begging her to come out to a restaurant for dinner. I want her to want to see the world. I want her to want. If she can still want, then we'll continue to move forward. I try to get her excited about the farmer's market. I tell her I need a sweater. I think of us in the past, walking downtown in the crisp Oregon fall, drinking coffee at outdoor tables and eating gyros. I cajole and repeat myself, but she shakes her head. And every time she says no to this, to me, it feels like my lungs are dipped in lead. "What would you want to eat if you could go out?" I finally asked her.

You cannot get shrimp with lobster sauce in Eugene. The Chinese restaurants here serve fried tempura or braised shrimp or shrimp nesting in greasy noodles, but the dish she most loves never appears on menus.

"No problem!" Ellen said when I mentioned it to her. She sounded thrilled to be invited up to the house; thrilled to do something for my mother.

"Here," she says, bending over me. I have the snow peas washed and in the colander. "Let me show you a trick." She takes a paring knife and cuts off the end of the pea, making it look like a little fish. I continue in this manner, creating a school of snow peas. The precision of this act soothes me. I could cut peas forever. We wash the rice. We lay out our ingredients in small bowls.

The last step, as we sizzle the shrimp in stock and cornstarch, is to spoon a dark sauce into the pan.

"That doesn't look right," I say when the white begins to turn a graying brown. The dish we're aiming for is white, all white, streaked with eggs. When you put it over rice, it vanishes. Ellen goes bloodless, then bends over the little book.

"Oh shit," she says. "There are two versions." We've ruined it. "We can wash it off," Ellen says, grabbing the handle of the wok. She wears the dull fearful hurt of the living in this house. None of us can ever do what it takes. We don't have the magic we know we need.

"No," I say. It's already night, too late.

I walk into the bedroom and wheel her out. We ladle up rice and shrimp. Ellen is apologizing. My mother gazes at the food.

"This is the nicest thing," she says. She looks at us as if we've handed her a plate of amethyst bracelets. Ellen continues to apologize and my mother looks at her, a look I know well, a look that makes her shut up.

It's another day again and we're having a hard time getting Mom to lie down. She can't breathe when she's horizontal—there's too much damage to her diaphragm and lung. When Barb caught wind of this, she suggested we get Mom a hospital bed—another service that hospice provides, beds with buttons so you can sleep sitting up, beds with railings so you can't get out of them. Today I moved the bedside tables so the guy could install it.

The guys from the medical supply place always smile wetly at me. I can never tell if they're flirting or simply trying to be nice, but thinking about it gives me something to do. Some days I smile back at them. Some days I try a wry, knowing look. Today, though, the young man doesn't look my way. He's humorless and ruddy and blond and carries in the metal parts, then the poles. He sets these at the foot of my mother's big cherrywood bed. Then he comes in with the mattress made of foam that remembers your body. My mother sits on the bed, watching, and I wait for her to crack a joke about the foam having a better brain than she does, but she's in her black baggy nightgown and she just stares wide-eyed at the man, who nearly knocks a painting off the wall as he whams springs and poles into place.

He will not look at us, my mother and me, and finally he is done.

"That's awful," my mother says. And for a long time we sit, staring at the railings.

A few days ago, the oxygen guys' truck broke down in front of our house. They were out there for a couple of hours, just sitting in the rare fall sunshine, listening to the radio. I went out to walk Mercy and of course she scooted over to them, wagging her tail wildly, rolling on her back, fainting. They petted her and made a fuss and said they loved dogs, especially ones that looked like coyotes. And Mercy jumped up and fainted again, grinding her back into the pavement. And the cute one looked up at me, right into my eyes, and in a quiet voice asked, "Is that your mom?" And I said yes. And he held my gaze and softly said, "I'm so sorry."

And on top of all this, Arthur is dying. Arthur was

supposed to be my childhood pet, though he always preferred my mother. He replaced Tinkerbell (named after the fairy, despite vehement eye-rolling by my mother), a pound cat that would hiss and spit the minute you came near her. If you ignored her warnings, she'd swiftly draw blood. "It's because you named her Tinkerbell," my mother would say.

When I was nine, we went on a family vacation and when we returned, Tinkerbell had disappeared. My father cackled delightedly and delivered graphic accounts of the housesitter's rager. He claimed she barbecued the cat, serving kitty riblets to her sorority sisters. I ignored him and made yellow signs that my mother hung around the neighborhood. Tinkerbell never returned and, after telling my dad to can the riblet joke, my mother researched friendly cat breeds and found Arthur, a Himalayan, in the local paper. Arthur's kittenhood is documented thoroughly in plastic albums in my bedroom. I was a girl obsessed with his puffy whiteness, his vacant blue eyes. There are photos of me in Long Island with my cousins, dressed in a long black sweatshirt with rhinestones studded over the neckline and shoulder pads (a gift, my mother insists, from my aunt), clamping a squirming Arthur to my chest. Photos of my mother eating a sandwich, objecting to the camera in her face, the kitten standing on her shoulder. As he grew older, the cat chose a spot under a ceramic lamp in the living room and sat there, paws crossed in front of him, for most of many years.

Now this patient cat is seventeen years old and he's locked in a bedroom downstairs with food and water and tomorrow morning, I'm pretty sure he will be dead. My mom's friend Melinda says the cat and my mother will go together but I think the cat is going to beat her. He's only bone under a thin skin and he doesn't move when you touch him anymore. When he stands, one side of his body collapses and he starts to convulse.

My dad thinks we should put the cat down and leave his body at the vet's, and maybe he's right, but I keep thinking that at this point we have to have more respect for death than that. At this point, we will have to bury that cat under a tree in the yard with cans of cat food coated in gold. Or it will seem like we haven't learned anything.

I'm sitting across from my mother in the kitchen, drinking coffee and reading about the humanitarian worker who was kidnapped in Iraq and the nine-year-old boy in Oregon who saw his stepdad kill his mother, when my mother says: "Oh no."

I look up and there's blood, bright against her soft lips, around the corners of her mouth. It's a nosebleed, thick as paint. And I run for the Kleenex and we try to stop it but she can't breathe without the tubes up her nose so we put them back and they begin to fill with blood, like celery when you put it in food coloring.

My dad is out doing errands; I have no idea how to get in touch with him. And it occurs to me that she could bleed to death at the table. Don't cancer patients die of nosebleeds all the time? Or that she could clog the tubes and not be able to breathe and die that way. And now she's going to die and I'm going to stand here and watch as she suffocates on a combination of tumors and blood.

But somehow she gets it to stop as I stand there, handing her Kleenex. And without seeming at all ruffled, she goes back to bed.

"I think you ought to change some of the doses." Barb has arrived with her bag of meds and her paperwork. She tries to look official, presiding over her notepad, shielding her clipboard from me every time I crane my neck to sneak a look (what *is* it that she writes on that thing?), but she just ends up looking bossy. It's crazy she's the usher of death, what with her bad bangs and jowly cheeks. Where are her sequined heels? The black velvet cape such an usher should wear? Barb has decided that we need to up Mom's pain medicine. Mom's not complaining of pain, but what's Barb to do with her bag of pills and patches? And Mom says okay, there is some radiating pain in her breast.

My mother's worn a pain patch for years. It sends gentle doses of a morphine derivative into her bloodstream. Barb takes out a second patch and instructs us that it needs to be put on in the middle of the cycle of the previous patch. We have a little day planner and we make notes about this. It is, apparently, crucial that we don't mess this up. But a day or two later, my father admits that he forgot when he administered the first patch. He stands over my mother with the gelatinous square of drug and scratches his cheek. "It was Tuesday, right? The day the bath aid came? Or was it Wednesday?" My mother stares at him, her brows raised.

You numbskull.

And there is this fact, too—a fact I can't decipher. My mother told me that she asked my father to list the things he will miss about her when she is gone. My father refused to answer.

"Why?" she asked.

"Stoppit," he said.

"Why?" she pushed. "I've been married to you for thirty-five years. You can't think of a few things?"

"Jackie, stop."

I can imagine what my mother wants him to say. She wants him to remember the big red tent they had on their honeymoon, the one with the shaded porch and walls for different rooms. She wants him to remember her sleeping in the sun on a grassy Swiss hillside. The sunburn she got in Mexico. She wants him to say he will miss the dinners, the salads with cucumbers, scallions, and tomatoes cut into wedges and the way she became irritated deveining shrimp. She wants him to remember her twenty-year-old skin, unblemished from surgeries and needles. The warm days after I was born and they felt they were the only ones in the world that had ever created a baby. She wants a catalog of trips they took, the daily comedies—like when they pretended to name a vizsla puppy Brick and went around the house yelling *Brick, Brick, here, Brick* until the dog was paralyzed with confusion and my mom couldn't breathe she was laughing so hard. She wants him to say how much he will miss talking to her about work, about the quality of salmon and possible vacations, about me. There are a million moments that will end the day she dies and she wants this acknowledged. She wants him to imagine the empty bed. And she wants him to appreciate that it's not yet empty.

But my father cannot meet her here. No matter how much she asks, cries, balls her fists.

"Why do you have to keep on with this?" he says.

"I need to talk to you," my mother says. She's sitting with the day planner at the kitchen table. She's pissed and scheming, and she's sulking a little. I take my juice and set it down, dramatically flinging myself into the wooden chair. "I can't trust your father," she says. She narrows her eyes as she looks at him, then widens them when she looks back at me. He's by the sink, of course, watching. "I need for *you* to be in charge of the medications."

My father pulls his lips tight. A weird kind of triumph sweeps over me.

Later we go into the bedroom so I can change her patch. She stands up and lifts her nightgown with shaking hands. I've not seen her rear in twenty years. It's plump and perky—the only part of her body that hasn't been wildly distorted. I smooth the patch down, careful to secure the edges. I try not to think about it. I look at the light fixtures, half-disks protruding from the wall, lighting sections of ceiling, leaving most of the room dim. And I think that I would like to die, right then, a flash of light, a burst of pain. Please. And just be spared.

In the morning, my father wakes me up to tell me he has to go out and I need to go sleep downstairs near my mother. I took two Xanax last night and I can't understand him at all, I'm slowly rising out of a fog, too slowly, he's already saying, *okay then,* and I know I've been given some instructions about the dogs and my mother and the phone but I have no idea what they are.

I walk downstairs to sleep in the pink bed of the spare room and it's full of grit from my dad's vizslas. I lie down and Mercy goes bananas, jumping all over me, playing tug-of-war with my hair. I want to cry; I'm still pretty fogged and I try to remember what those training books said. I flip her on her back and growl at her, but I'm too tired to sound convincing, my eyes are half closed, and who's convincing in a pink tank top and purple underwear? She thinks I'm playing and twists out from under me, flying off the bed barking, racing around the room.

An hour later I hear my mother screaming. "ROBIN ROBIN!" I jump out of bed and run into the kitchen.

"What?" I'm still in my underwear, ready to perform valiant acts, ready to cut a hole through her trachea like I've seen on television or stanch bleeding with baking soda.

"Your alarm clock is going off," she says. "And I need the morphine from my bathroom." My heart sends little pinpricks to my fingers as I calm down and walk upstairs to shut off the beeping, pull on pants and a sweater. I check on the dying cat on my way to find the morphine. He's lying on his side. I kneel over to see if he's alive and place my hand on his cool body. He lifts his head, drags himself over to the water, and drinks.

Then I get the dropper bottle and go back to the kitchen to fix up the nebulizer. My mom can't hold it still to puff from it; she's shaking like mad, jerking. She can't talk, either, and when I ask her a question she just looks angry and waves her hand in my face.

On the playground of Harris Elementary, Becca Hamill educated me about sex. We were in the first grade and Becca had it out for the deaf girl, Ella. I don't recall seeing Ella inside the school, but at recess she always turned up, making the loudest noises and slamming boys on the heads and backs with a fist bedecked in a rhinestone-studded glove. Ella terrified me, but she irritated Becca, and every time Ella came by, Becca stuck her middle finger through a hole she made with her thumb and forefinger. Becca explained that this gesture meant fucking. At Becca's house, during sleepovers, we would bounce up and down on her twin bed, watching the stuffed animals fly off and hit the floor, and Becca would freeze and say *shhhhh. Shhhhhhhh*. She'd take my hand and we'd stand in front of her parents' door and she'd claim she could hear the fucking sounds.

I never heard anything.

There were books, too. Since this was a hippie town, stray copies of *Where Did I Come From?* found their way to slumber parties. We all claimed to be grossed out, though who wasn't secretly enthralled with the pictures, the pubic hair drawn on like grass? Of course, we also attended sex ed in the fifth grade, where Lance, our young redheaded teacher, drew our questions from a shoe box. When he drew the question "What does sex feel like?," he sat on his stool for a very long time. His face turned a brighter shade than his hair and he squinted at the faded science posters.

"It feels . . . totally . . . incredible," he said. The class fell into an awed silence.

My mom missed the boat. By the time she'd decided to sit me down for a sex talk, I'd finished fifth grade and knew all there was to know about foreplay and orgasm. However, she had no idea how sophisticated I'd become and I never dreamed of telling her.

We took a family trip to Hawaii. Ordinarily, my mother and I might journey down to the pool. She'd lie on a beach chair, a floppy hat on her head, large sunglasses making her look like a bug. She'd order a chi-chi and I'd order a virgin chi-chi and we'd *relax*. But today she had other ideas.

"Come, let's sit on the patio," she said, heading for her suitcase where much to my dismay, I'd seen a suspicious-looking book. Beige and textbooky, it had slender script on the cover alongside a photograph of a smiling mother and daughter. My mother had on her teacher face—a phony pertness in her brow and nose. She was going to educate me, talk to me about *sexual intercourse* in a high tone, like she was reading to me about *Botswana, Mozambique*. She was going to, in typical Mom fashion, talk about sex like it was geography.

I fidgeted in the plastic chair.

"Do you want to read aloud?" she asked, her voice melodious, aggravating. I became acutely aware of the dirt under the weave in the plastic furniture.

"I already know this stuff," I muttered. She waited.

Then, with a carefree shrug, she began to read, pronouncing each word with painful accuracy. I clipped and unclipped the seashell barrette that held up one side of my hair. I'd seen a group of girls on the beach and felt desperate to find them, to get a tan, to get away from my mom.

I thought we were done when we reached the last section but, to my horror, my mother alighted on the *Ideas* page. An Idea: Bring a set of colored pencils to your talk and, as a parent-child team, color in the larger-than-life illustrations of the *fallopian tubes,* the *labia,* the *clitoris.* My mother, rigid with goodwill, reached into her straw bag and pulled out a set of Crayola pencils.

"Mom," I gasped.

"What?" she said, too loud, coloring in the clitoris lightly.

Blue. I haven't forgotten that detail.

We've migrated to the living room. Lily loves the loose weave of my mother's fancy upholstery and little loops of thread stick out all over, where she has clawed. I finger a loop, try to fit it back inside the tiny square hole it's left. But my mom's eyes are humming, she's focused on my face. "Will you do it for me?" she asks. I shrug and give up on the loop.

It turns out to be a false request. I have no choice. I'm *going* to speak to the rabbi. He parks his Subaru in front of the house, blocking the mailbox. The mailman keeps getting pissed about this (*what's with all these CARS),* but my mom says, sweetly, that the mailman can go fuck himself. I watch Yitzak climb the wooden steps slowly, as if his heels are made of concrete. He carries a prayer book under his arm.

My father's gone out, so it's just my mother, the rabbi, and me in the sunken formal living room. On normal days, two wooden chairs block the entry so that the dogs don't pee on the thick wool rug. My mother's back is rigid. The rabbi sits next to her, places his hand on her shoulder. I can't look at him.

"How are you doing, Jackie?" he almost whispers. My mother's eyes fill with tears. Three large windows look over the Subaru and the blocked mailbox and I wish I could float out toward them, down the hill, into the trees. My mother tells him that she's stopped treatment, that she's afraid, afraid for me. That I am not talking to anyone. The rabbi looks at me. I look into the whorls of paint in the closest painting. A girl with a violin. Her face is distorted, melonlike. Inside the gray of her dress I can see blue and orange and green. I can even see the little ridges the hair of the paintbrush left in each stroke.

"Do you have any questions for Yitz?" my mother asks. I feel her trying to bring me back, closer to her. She wants me to grab on to something, a buoy, a rope. Everyone keeps trying to throw me a rope, but there's never a rope there when I look, just blue, just air.

"Well," my mother says. She keeps adjusting the way she's sitting. One of her slippers comes off and I watch her try to scoot it back on her foot. The slipper eludes her, inching slowly into the middle of the rug. Finally, I get up and grab it for her, stick it back on.

"Can you tell us, in Judaism, what happens to people when they die?" she asks. I feel a pressure in my chest. She's asking this for me, she wants me to have this, something to think, someplace to look for her when she leaves me. I look straight at Yitz's face. Such an old face for a youngish man. He is trying to reach me with his eyes, but I harden mine. He will not get in.

Yitz nods slowly and then looks away from me, out at the big pine tree in front of the house, out at his practical car. "There is a great energy in the universe," he says, his cheeks hollow, his beard so still. He tries to empty himself, to ready himself for something deep and beautiful to come flooding in. "And when you die, you rejoin this great energy."

I feel so many things at once, but most strongly I feel the overwhelming need to laugh. This is it? This is what you learn after years of rabbinical training, prayer, study of the rituals that make us human? That we join up with energy? No castles? No devils or angels? Just a *feeling*? Ha! Hahaha! How ridiculously accurate and perfect! How *great*!

Earlier this spring, the latest experimental treatment stopped working. The cells warped inside my mother, traveled to her liver, hovered around her lungs. I came home every other weekend and we would settle into the sofa and night would fall around us. My father went off to sleep, tangled in dogs, and my mother and I would watch interior design shows, rating the cleverness of transforming the console into two nightstands. And sometimes we would feel brave. Sometimes I would cry.

"What?" she would say. Some nights I couldn't talk,

58

I could only sit there, paralyzed. Eventually, though, I spoke.

"There are so many things I want to know."

"Ask me. Ask me *now*, Robin." Usually I couldn't handle the intensity of these moments. I would shake my head and feel the hurt in my throat become my throat, until even my skin radiated with pain. She would stare at me, wanting to help me. But I was too afraid that if I got the answers, it would be okay for her to die.

Then I did ask. I wasn't sure what I wanted to know, but I made an awkward list and read it to her. "I want to know the timeline of your life, the years you studied abroad, when you got your master's at Columbia. I want to know what it feels like to be pregnant. I want to know what you and Dad used to talk about when you were young."

She sat, trying to think.

"I was a child when I met your father," she told me. Neither of them can remember when they met, which has always puzzled and disappointed me. "I used to sit in the library while he studied. He never felt smart enough, he always thought he needed to study more than anyone else. Sometimes I made him good luck cards. I was never very artistic, though."

I have my mom's homemade cards upstairs, under my bed. My father's mother gave them to me; she'd kept them for almost thirty-five years under the record player. "Take, them," she said, handing me the crumbling manila envelope. "No one else wants them." They are painfully sweet construction paper cutouts of flowers and butterflies, inside jokes written in perfect curvy penmanship.

My penmanship, to the tee—it's true.

One night, sitting there under the old crocheted afghan, she said, "I get so angry at this disease. Sometimes I think if I can just hold on to you, it won't be able to take me. If I can just hold on tight enough, I won't die."

When she said this, a pain started in my lower back and traveled into my leg. I spent the next day holed up in bed on a heating pad, popping pain pills, but nothing would make it go away.

On Thursday we put the cat, Arthur, to sleep and left his body at the vet's. It's Monday now and we have forgotten about the poor cat, his silent suffering, the way his eyes sank into his gray face, the blueness of them turned cold and remote and full of water. When I picked him up, his fur was matted with filth and he meowed so loudly. And yesterday I threw away the World's Biggest Litter Box that we'd made for him, the giant storage container that he still peed outside of, and I felt so matter-of-fact about it, which makes me feel like a coldhearted person, when really, my heart is so big it has become unfamiliar to me, I am drowning in all its redness, I can barely breathe and see, it's so swollen and raw from expansion.

My father and I sit, staring at the television, when I realize that I neglected to deal with Mercy's staples. I get on the rug and roll her over, petting her ears with one hand while I poke and prod her belly with the other. Is she going to die now? Will the staples come loose inside her? How could I have forgotten this? My neck starts to ache and I'm nearly in a panic when my dad looks down. "I can take those out," he says. We find a pair of clippers and wander upstairs into the bathroom by the loft. I hold Mercy down while my father sterilizes the clippers with an ancient bottle of rubbing alcohol.

When I was little, he sometimes took me to the hospital with him while he did rounds. He'd sit me in the nurses' station in front of the heart monitors. "Check to make sure none of the lines go flat," he'd say. A serious child, I would do as told, my blood pressure rising every time a series of bumps grew smaller. Now I watch him hunched over the dog, ever the doctor. It's a crude process. He snips at the dog's belly and the sharp little staples go flying around the tile. Finally, he's done. We sit back and Mercy leaps up and races away. We run our hands over the floor, but we can't find all the staples. "Wear shoes in here," my father says. He drops the clippers on the counter.

When I first arrived here to a mother whose fingers were not blue, when it dawned on me that I would be staying here for more than four days, that I needed to drop out of graduate school, that I needed to tell my roommate to send me my mail and pay the bills, I found an ad for a nine-week dog-training class, taught on Monday nights just outside of town. Though I'd read dog books obsessively, Mercy was a deeply enthusiastic animal and I couldn't stop her from jumping on everyone who came through the door.

"Should I do it?" I asked my father. He was eating a melon over the sink, the way he always eats melon—cut in half, scooping the innards out with a teaspoon. The dead cat, in his glory days, used to wait beside the sink so he could eat the melon seeds my dad left strewn all over the porcelain. Then my mother would walk in to find the melon carcass, the happy cat, and she would say proudly, "This family is disgusting."

"Why not?" he asked, slurping an orange spoonful.

"It's nine weeks long," I said. "Do you think I'll still be here?" We both knew what I meant by this. He lowered the melon and looked at me. Then he turned back to the melon.

"You should do it," he said.

The first class is a dog-free class and my dad agrees to come along. "Maybe I'll train Sol," he jokes. Sol careens through the house, growling at Mercy, making her cower in submission. He drapes himself on the sofa, on the bed, refusing to move if you shove him. He would never growl at you; he won't stoop to that level. He simply makes himself too heavy to shove and you lose.

We pull up in the deserted industrial parking lot. The teacher greets us as we open the heavy doors and she immediately alarms me. Something is wrong with her head. Lines of pink cover her cheeks, like skid marks made from tiny cars, and bumps cover her nose and chin. She's the wrong colors—gray, taupe, ruddy red. Her voice makes all of this worse. It sounds like it's being thrown to her by a ventriloquist. I can't take my eyes off her.

My father and I sit in the bleachers, staring at Sue. We've left Mom with Suzanne. Free to be anywhere in the world, we're here in a gym, on bleachers, the freezing air coming in through the drafty roof, watching this woman demonstrate a clicker, the right kind of leash clasp. She has words for everything—*kong, liver treat, puzzle ball*—and she speaks these words the way Barb speaks about drugs. There's nothing hospice-lavender here, however. Here, everything is red.

She hands us our course reader. I open it to find that she can't spell. Her list of Top Ten Secrets is actually a list of "Secretes" in bold, like commands. SECRETE #1, she commands. SECRETE #2.

"Secrete number one," I whisper to my dad. "Secrete number two!" But he doesn't crack a smile.

She begins to tell us how the clicker works. Dogs don't learn the way we learn, she says. If you click your clicker at the moment the dog does something good, then treat the dog with liver, the dog will begin to associate the click with the treat. The click will link up to the action. If you wait and run for a treat when the dog sits, the dog will lose sight of what it did. But if you keep the clicker with you on a cord around your neck, you can click, then run for the treat. This is because you get straight to the dog's *amygdala* this way. My father has been staring at the dust motes near the light high above us, deep in his private dimension, so it surprises me when he's suddenly completely present next to me, his eyes alight.

"An amygdala?" my dad whispers. "Did she make that up?" For the rest of the session he nudges me every time Sue says *amygdala*. She keeps saying it. *Amygdala, amygdala,* and by the end, I am shaking with silent tears.

Sue glares at us as we leave. "Amygdala," my dad whispers and this sends me into another fit of giggles.

Barb appears again. I don't keep track of her schedule, so finding her in the kitchen feels similar to finding a roach. My mother crosses her ankles above the metal footrests of the wheelchair. This morning I shoved her swollen feet into clean white socks and now they look swaddled and safe. "On a scale of one to five, Jackie, five being unbearable pain, how much pain do you feel?" Barb asks.

My mother stares at her blankly. "Two. I don't know. Six." Barb stares blankly back.

"Six," Barb finally says, and writes it down. My mom looks at the corner of the dark wood on the window frame. The pieces don't square exactly; there is a small slice of darkness.

"Sure," she says.

"How's the medication?" she wants to know. "Should we up the doses?" My mother shrugs again and Barb writes something down in her file. "You know," Barb says, "it's quite possible that the breast will split open from tumor." Very matter-of-fact, she is, but when she looks at my mother, she makes her therapist face, her mouth turned down and eyes too big. "The tumor can outgrow the interior area," she says, softening the words slightly so they sound more babyish. My mother's face goes totally white. She doesn't say anything. She turns and looks at the wall.

After this, Barb wheels my mom into the bedroom. When my mom permits, Barb gets to practice "healing touch." I've seen her do it. She turns on some kind of tribal music and looks like a mime running her palms over a fake glass cocoon. I know the look on her face is supposed to be reverence, but it's so tight that she just looks constipated. Today my dad and I don't watch. We sit in the living room and drink iced tea. We need to rest.

I sleep in the front bedroom so my father can go out in the morning to hike and I will be able to hear my mother if she calls. But he never goes hiking and when I go into her bedroom that morning, his face hangs grayly and his eyes are red and he is a tiny man, shrunken and weak. His lips seem made of rice paper, like they will wear away and chafe off and his pinkness is the thing that will come through all the spaces, his pinkness out of his eyes and his mouth and his lips.

"It was a terrible night," he says. My mom is in bed now, strapped to her mask, a little angel.

"What happened?" I ask.

"The mask broke, I couldn't figure it out, I kept repeating the same thing over and over and I was too tired to realize I couldn't fix it and the oxygen guy came at four and then we didn't test it and he came back at five and I didn't get any sleep. It was hell. She was totally disoriented and every time I turned around, she'd torn the mask from her face."

I sit next to her sleeping body. I agree to sit here, just sit, while my father takes the dogs up the mountain. I watch her breathe, the rising and falling of her chest a small miracle. It's as if the mask is funneling something into her body—something more important than oxygen.

My mother struggled with her weight over the years. Her mother put her on a diet when she was two years old. She speaks of this rarely, hurt in her voice. She never served steamed vegetables because, apparently, she'd been forced to eat them as part of this baby dieting and the smell makes her queasy. Her fear of the camera means that few photographs of her as an adult exist. However, on my twenty-first birthday, two years into the cancer, she made me an album. I didn't understand the gift at the time. She usually gave me earrings or a bracelet and the album felt weighty, sentimental. The first pages are baby pictures of my mother and father and me, all bald and helpless in our baby jammies. And then, there she is, young and radiant, thin as a twig, holding a tiny red me, gazing down at the swaddled lump, a sheen of peace and optimism on her face. Her hair is short and pixie-ish, almost black, her cheeks are flushed. She rocks me in an unfinished wooden rocker. I was born two weeks early, a girl instead of the boy they anticipated, and the preparations were not complete. The pictures of my mother holding me as a baby are some of the happiest pictures I have ever seen. I am dazed and awestruck, staring at the weird shapes of the world, and she looks like she is going to go tearing through the paper of the picture in a fit of white-toothed euphoria. But a few pages later, the photos are only of me—a sad-eyed toddler with a gaping purple scar beneath my eye from a dog bite, my copper hair like silk antennae. And then I am a dark-haired, deeply tanned eight-year-old in a pink tutu made by my mother's mother, somber and serious as I practice my ballet moves near a potted ficus. And my mother's cursive writes about each phase of my life. At two years old, they took me to a farm to find a pumpkin for Halloween and there are about ten photographs of me dragging pumpkins out of a crate, combing the bins for the perfect shape. Years later, my mother would take me shoe shopping and grow aggravated by the way I studied the shoe, picky about the color of the thread that bound the sole to the leather. Her words above the pumpkin photos: *You always had discriminating taste, even then.*

But my favorite pages are the ones where she documents my love of fashion. "Who was this child of mine?" my mother writes, "with her love of whimsy and flair for fashion—and her incredible sense of fun?" And there I am, bedecked in all sort of insane outfits. A four-year-old in footed pajamas with a turquoise Tupperware bowl as a hat and a mink stole. A little older, thinking I am hilarious in a bright red nightgown and matching cap, worn with reading glasses stolen from my grandmother, my nose a button under the giant frames. And in high school the outfits turned to vintage dresses—gauzy with flowers or butterflies, worn over jeans with beaded sweaters and work boots. There's a photograph of me speaking at my high school graduation (before Ken Kesey, whom I lured into speaking, too), in a red velvet and gold lamé 1960s minidress with a garland of dried roses in my shiny straight hair.

Sometimes I'd come down from the loft and she'd

exclaim, "What is that schmata?" But by the time I was a senior in high school, she'd decided to go with it. She'd smile as I wore crimson velvet with a Pendleton and she'd admire my originality. She claims this came from the sky, the way the traits of children sometimes do. But I think it comes down the line of women in her family. My grandmother used to say I got my love of style from her mother, Yetta, whose husband, Jack, imported ostrich feathers when hats were in vogue, who built the first movie theater in Panama and had grand plans for their future. (Unfortunately, he was run over by a car on the Fourth of July, leaving Yetta widowed and poor in her forties.) Yetta, in every photograph before Jack died, is buttoned into fitted jackets, her hair curling gently, the feathers flying from her hats. Her brooches and hat-pins sparkle. Her petticoats bell out the fabric on her long skirts. While my mother might not have been an adventurous dresser, she had particular fashion sense. In a town where everyone wears jeans and Gortex, my mother wore lined skirts with dark hose, little scarves and wildly patterned blouses. She always curled her lashes, her shoes never looked scuffed.

I sit with Mercy on the bed, and together we page through the album. I'm in the same green shirt I've been wearing for days. I didn't pack anything for a day out. The only feather I've seen is the one woven into the skylight upstairs. And it has been weeks since I've seen my mother in anything but a nightshirt. Months since she's packed her red leather bucket bag with a wallet, keys. My mother and I might as well be wearing dark shrouds. We are too preoccupied to rummage through our closets to find the perfect combination of silver and brown. We are becoming something else, something quieter, something unfettered, something darker, a period of mother-daughterhood not documented in the album.

The day I arrived here with Don, he took a few photographs of my mother and me on the sofa. She's gray and drugged. A crocheted afghan covers her legs and the oxygen tubes dangle from her nose. I smile and lean into her as if trying to make like it's going to be all right. I look almost radiant, like if I smile hard enough I can normalize this tragedy, I can convince everyone, including death, that we are FINE. And she leans toward me, in profile, her eyes lidding over. She holds my head as she kisses my cheek and in this photo she looks like she knows something, like she is sending a message through my skin.

It's an eerie photograph. I keep it in the diary I don't write in. I got this film developed so I'd have some photos of Don and was shocked to find this one at the end of the roll. Every time I look at it, I feel I can almost see through her.

"Oh," Barb says on the phone to me later that day when I tell her how much worse it got, how she was up all night, ripping her oxygen mask off every time my father turned away, until she finally broke it; how he spent the night making phone calls and keeping my mother in bed, holding the mask to her face. "I doubled the Atavan before I left," Barb tells me calmly. "She just seemed so anxious."

Is this a movie about narcotics? Is this a *Just Say No* campaign?

That's no problem, I want to say, but the next time you decide to overmedicate my mother in secret it would be great if you'd bring your pajamas and hunker down. We'll watch some DVDs under the afghans and eat popcorn and do facials and when my mom gets up and rips the BiPAP off because she can't remember what it's doing on her face and then can't make it to the bathroom, we can be a team! We can clean it up together, recounting the movie, taking breaks to sing little songs from our childhoods.

"I think she's overmedicated," I say.

"She was in such *pain,*" Barb says, her voice rising. "She's really suffering, she told me so."

She told me so.

I hang up and my father walks around the corner.

"Who was that?"

"Barb," I say. "She says it's not the double fentanyl dose, it's that she gave Mom a second Atavan before she left because Mom seemed anxious. She just forgot to mention it." I know my eyes are wide and my nostrils all the way open. I am about to go flinging out of my skin. This doesn't seem like a difficult thing to do, to fling out of one's skin. Why people are not always flinging in and out of their skin is a mystery to me! "Are you anxious? Because maybe she can bring over a vat of morphine for the whole family!" My dad's face goes grim for a moment. He seems disturbed. He opens his mouth and I'm sure he's about to doctor-logic me about Barb, tell me that medicine is a rough science, you have to use your judgment even though sometimes you are simply wrong. But then he laughs. He grabs my shoulders, pulls me to him, and thunks me on the back with his thick hand.

My mother is the only person ever to love me selflessly and she is dying. I need someone to drop everything, to come running. The only possibility I have, the one person on my list, is Don.

Over the summer, Don came for a week. We took walks by the river and drove to the coast where we ate chowder and looked at the sea lions swimming in a bay. Don likes Eugene. The size of it comforts him. You can always park at the grocery. If you need echinacea, you don't have to wait twenty minutes in line at Whole Foods, you just drive down the hill to the wooden natural food shack. You can sit for hours under a tree by the roar of a current, paging through books, unrushed, undisturbed.

But this time, he's not so interested in coming to stay.

"Can you take some time off?" I ask. I have been pressuring him, asking him over and over, in a million different ways. Come and be with me. He doesn't respond. I imagine the muscles in his jaw tensing and releasing. His greeny-blue eyes, open and vulnerable so much of the time, would have their flicker of meanness, of coldness that comes with this kind of quiet.

"I really need you here," I say. I'm sure desperation has seeped into my tone, but how can I communicate it to someone who has not lived through a single day of this dying? How do I tell him about the blisters on my mother's face? The swelling of her arms and feet? The CD I spotted in the stereo, brought by Barb: *Music for a Gentle Passing*? How do I convince him that at the end of the day my arms and legs, fingers and toes are not attached to my body? That they have been flung around the house, that I can't find them, that I am just a heart beating slowly, that I need him to help me gather the pieces, to put one hand on either side of me and make sure I get, at the very least, from one hour to the next.

"I have bills, Robin. I have a job. What would it look like if I just left? I can't just leave. I've already taken too much time off." I remind him that, just a few weeks ago, he chose to use his airline voucher to go to New York, not Oregon.

"That was something I needed to do for *me*," he says. "I still exist, too, Robin. Your life is not the only one that matters." He's so angry. I'm so angry. He claims he can't take time off because he won't have rent money and so I've offered to help him. Whatever it takes. I'll figure it out. But then it's his loans and we both know that money is not the real issue. He doesn't *want* to come. This woman who winces in pain, who stares at the nebulizer with hate and longing, who shakes and shakes and shakes—this is *my* mother. *My* problem. He has a mother, a life, a job, friends. He has his own problems.

"You could leave. Your boss gives you everything you ask for." If I continue with this, he'll hang up.

"I'm on the phone with you more than once a day, Robin. We talk constantly. I'm here for you. You know that. I can't do everything you tell me just because you tell me to do it. I'm not a dog."

As if she hears him, Mercy lifts her head. She's been glued to my side for weeks. I run my hand the wrong way up her fur, scratching her with my fingernails. She quivers and groans, sits up and faces me, then collapses against my side.

He is here for me. I hear this, over and over again. My friends say it, too, over voice mail. *Here for you. Here for you.*

What does this mean? When I hang up, I'm alone. I put my cold fingers into the corners of my eyes and press until a pressure feels relieved. I drag my bare heels against the carpet until they burn. There is a part of me, a part I try to ignore, that could drag my heels over the rough nap until they bleed, that wants to leave streaks of blood over the carpet that no one comes up here to see. He is not here for me. No one but my mother is here for me.

She is the only one.

I don't discuss Don, rarely invoke him here. Occasionally someone asks after him and the answers are curt. When I go back to Berkeley, after this is done, maybe he'll make sense again. He is part of that world of people in their twenties. Part of the jobs and bills and trips and restaurants and breakups. But right now he is the ghost boyfriend of a ghost me—and both of us are beside the point.

By the time he agrees to come for a lightning-fast visit (two nights, not the duration, not three weeks, not even one), I half hate him. Perhaps you can't expect your boyfriend to stop his life, to come running, to cook soups and make beds. Aside from my father, this house is filled with women. Women stop their lives; they're programmed that way. A child comes into the world and suddenly the choices grow fewer. The women seem to understand the payoff. You sacrifice, yes. You don't get to the gym, to the shrink, to the office, but you get this fragment of a moment with a person who is momentary, who will not be like this again.

"You guys should get away for a night," Martha says. "You should stay at a hotel, just get some rest, see the regular world." I listen, completely disinterested. If I leave for a night, who's to say my mother will survive it? We brush up against the end every day. Even going to the store for bread gives me anxiety. The ticking of the clock has gotten so loud.

But they go in on it together, Martha and Suz. They pool their money and get us a room at a Victorian bed-and-breakfast near their law firm. When Don arrives in his little rental car that evening, we pack up and go.

"Is this it?" he says. Big trees line the driveway. We come to a clearing where a few other cars sit in front of a carriage house. The main building is shingled, white with hunter green trim. Light blares from all the windows, as if to tell us that inside the lobby, families sit bathed in firelight, drinking hot cocoa and playing board games. Don walks very straight, pleased to have a night in a bed-and-breakfast, a little vacation from his hectic city life. He likes hotels and we almost never have the luxury. He likes breakfasts prepared for him by people who are paid to cook, eggs in dishes, toast on plates with little jars of jam. I can't begrudge him this. These things are nice. But when the man shows us our room— down a flight of steps obscured by flora, next to a man-made fountain that gurgles politely beside ornate white patio furniture, my hands feel angry. They seem to have a life of their own and I have to clasp them to get them to stay still.

We have to launch ourselves into the high bed. The mattress comes up to my chest. Different shiny floral patterns enhance the curtains, bedspread, and chairs. Silk tassels hang from the lamp shades. Lace edges the towels. Don starts rooting through the drawers as soon as the man leaves. He finds a VCR and some tapes. A movie starring Rosie Perez. I'm glad to have the television. A way of speeding through time. If there's quiet, I will think only of my mother, whether she is still alive, whether this time is just time I am not spending with her. She and I planned to take a trip to New Orleans, a mother-daughter trip, just for fun. We wanted to walk the old streets and see the hanging vines, hear music in a smoky club. But I spent too long pretending things were fine, working jobs and using my vacation time to travel to France with a boy. I never did it; she never pushed. She must have seen time running out, the ribbon of possibilities getting shorter and shorter. Sometimes I felt it in her silent watchfulness and it made my heart beat too fast, made my blood feel full of cool crystals.

I unwrap a candy.

In bed, later, I unscrew the top of the whiskey I brought. I pour it as if it's apple juice, into the thin transparent cups. When Don puts a hand on my back, I don't respond. I can't respond. That night, I have bad dreams, confusing dreams that have me awake at dawn, feeling like there's warm sand in my eyes, feeling nauseated. I'm sure that my mother has died, sure that because I was here in this overheated floral room, the white marble mantel glaring at me, I have missed the final moments and everyone else will have been there, been there for her while I drank whiskey on a ridiculous sleigh bed.

I'm relieved when it's finally morning. I call home, and Martha says: no news. Don and I walk to the little dining room in the main building and pretend, for just an hour, to be a young couple in weekend clothes (for me: same green T-shirt and jeans), out enjoying Eugene. I poke my poached eggs and watch the bright yellow stream through the excess water into the bread. I'm so relieved when we finish and the waiter takes away the plates.

"Do you want to go to the river?" Don asks. The river used to be my place, my refuge. I'd end up there every weekend, spreading a towel over sharp grass, faithfully toting inner tubes, bags of chips, novels and notebooks. We, the local kids, prided ourselves in being able to navigate the treacherous current, the muddy bottom, and decaying sunken logs strayed from clear-cuts up the mountains. But if we go now, I know I will hear something else. A dark sigh emerging from a black snake of water. Every summer a few kids die here, trapped by the arms of branches, held beneath the surface until they, too, are river. And I cannot watch the water rush by me.

"You can," I say. "But I need to go home."

On the way up the hill, I reach into the red leather bucket purse, made in Italy, that I filched from my mother's closet yesterday. It's her favorite bag and she'd never have let me use it if she had a shred of awareness. But for some reason, though the bag looks completely absurd with my grubby T-shirt and stained jeans, I'd wanted to take it with me. I'd emptied out its contents—her wallet and pens, receipts and business cards. And I'd packed it up with my uglier wallet, my wad of keys with the lobster bottle opener dangling from it. My hand, as I shove it in, gets all wet. At first, this doesn't register, but then I realize I'd tossed in a bottle of water and it has opened, filling the vinyl lining. The bag is so well made that the water has not seeped out. I extract my keys, wallet, phone. I focus on drying out the bag, wiping it with my shirt. If my mother notices I've ruined her fancy Italian bag, she will rally just long enough to kill me. When I get back to the house, I don't put the bag back. I want her to notice. I want her to need her wallet and realize the bag's gone missing. So I stick it upstairs near my bed.

It's night, the bathroom is a mess. The red rugs are bunched and wadded tissues dot the tile around them. Bottles of pills litter the counter. Toothpaste, bandages, wet washcloths. Don went by himself to the river, and I spent the afternoon dividing up the medications into the big pill organizer Barb brought. It's lavender, of course, and is divided into the sections of a day: morning, mid-morning, afternoon, evening, and bedtime. And it's as random as all the other divisions Barb has introduced, this idea about the day. We slide from night to afternoon to midmorning then back from midmorning to night and the world allows this but the pillbox does not. The pillbox is quite clear. It says: There Shalt Be Order in These Dark Times. Barb has also brought a purple pill cutter. I slide the little disks under the plastic blade and sever them with a click.

And now it's night in this bathroom full of glass and mirrors and deep orange terry cloth against white tile and I am handing my mother her drugs. She reaches out her hand and it's shaking and I put the shiniest one in first. Red and white like a big oval peppermint. She quivers and jerks and slowly gets it into her mouth. Then I lift the water and she swallows. She can barely talk now and she reaches for the other five pills. Usually her eyes are unfocused, wandering around the wall, the floor. But now she's staring as if to bring the pills to her mouth by telekinesis. I hand her one small yellow one but she objects and so I hand them all to her and she holds them in a wad in her fist and brings them to her mouth.

She's been taking all these pills for years—or most of them. The new drugs are the ones in liquid form: morphine, oxycodone, and the patches. She used to swallow them in private. I had a sense she took a lot of drugs; she'd start to float away in front of the eleven o'clock news. Before the drugs, night was our time. After my father went to sleep and she straightened the kitchen, I'd come and sit on the sofa, ask her for advice or tell her the latest gossip. We'd decide what we thought of family members or marriages, nail polish colors or styles of dining room chairs. We'd talk about my future, what I wanted to make of it, how to save money, how scary it felt to quit my government job in order to write. My mother would always listen and dispense practical solutions, staying up way past midnight with me—until we were both high on our second winds. We both liked this time, this little hole we carved in the night, on the sofa, the television muted, no one awake to hear us. But in the last few years, these nights have shifted. I might come downstairs and sit next to her, start telling her a story about a friend's new boyfriend only to notice that her head has fallen sideways. "Mom!" I'll say. But she's someone else. Her speech is slurred, like there's something large in her mouth, and she can't keep her jaw hinged shut. Once I came downstairs for a glass of water and found her bathed in the light of the refrigerator, eating peanut butter out of the jar, unable to answer questions. Fear became anger and I tried to be stern. "Mom, go to bed," I said. She smiled, her teeth coated in brown goo. Then, she took the jar under her robe and stuck her tongue out at me like a child. Twice, she fell.

I used to get angry with her for this. I was slowly being robbed of my mother through the evils of cancer—was she going to compromise what was left with narcotics? But every year the doctors added a few more drugs to the cocktail. Ambien then Atavan then Valium and Percocet. After all, she was slated to die and the doctors didn't have to follow her home, they didn't try to stay up remembering their childhoods with her. To the doctors, these drugs softened the harshness of living, numbed the patient against the disturbing questions. No one thought to check the charts, to see if they were overdoing it, to see what other doctors had prescribed. And it didn't take long before my mother was hooked, before she needed a new kind of pill to mute out the questions. Another recurrence meant another pill. Tumors enlarging meant a rise in dosage. Now after she takes the pills, I understand I won't be able to reach the mom I used to know.

I stand next to her as she runs water next to her toothbrush. With great concentration, she gets it to her mouth where she mashes it around. She refuses to look at herself in the mirror. When she does catch a glimpse, she almost always shrinks away, gasping.

Tonight she wears the rose-colored nightgown and it brings out the purples that have begun to flower under her eyes. Her skin is going lifeless, though she still occupies it. It's turning a doughy gray.

Who takes over the bodies of the dying? My mother was a civil rights attorney. She wore bright red lipstick and heavy gold necklaces. Her eyes defied regular notions of brown. They were brown spoked with gold light, full of judgment and sarcasm and a deep, harsh pleasure. She used to stand here in the mornings with a curling iron steaming, with gels and mousses and mascaras and little pressed circles of eye shadow. She was efficient. First she'd apply her foundation with a little white sponge, then blush with a large flowery brush, then eye shadow with steady strokes of her hand. She'd open her mouth wide to apply the eyeliner and mascara, finishing the job with a metal eyelash curler. And finally she got to the project of her hair. Now all these tools are put away in drawers.

She totters away from the sink, tugs her oxygen tubes through the doorway, toward the bed. It's so hard to get her settled. First we have to switch from the cannula to the mask, which involves a terrifying minute when the tubes must be disconnected and reconnected to other tubes. Done incorrectly, my mom won't be able to breathe. When she lies down (she hates the hospital bed, won't use it), she feels like she's drowning, and now she's hurt her back, pulled a muscle so that as she's reclining a shrieking pain goes through her and her face contorts. It takes us twenty minutes to get her in what appears to be a hellish heap on her side. I pull the covers over her and touch her soft cheek.

I go back upstairs. Don's in bed, reading, a glass of water standing beside him on the nightstand. I lie down next to him, put my hand on his rib cage and feel briefly comforted. I pick up a dog training book I haven't been reading. Don shifts so he can have his arm around me. His shirt smells of detergent. I read the same paragraph four times and decide to stare at the skylight instead.

An hour later, the call button rings. She's sitting up. I'm frustrated. It's going to take twenty more minutes to get her down again.

"Are you okay? Mom? Let's lie down." Her mouth hangs open and her eyes are shut. She won't respond.

"Mom," I repeat.

I put my hands on her shoulders to try to push her toward the mattress, but it's as if she's made of stone. "You need to lie down, Mom. You can't just sit here like this. You'll fall." She won't budge. But I can't let her sit, she'll keel over and bang her head on the metal railings of the useless hospital bed. I reach over to press the little gray pad on the intercom. "Dad, can you come here?"

Don pokes his head in. "Is everything okay?" he asks. He looks frightened and thin in the dark doorway. It's not his place, not his pain. This can't become his war story. He can't get to heaven faster by coming here for one weekend.

"Go," I snap. He backs away.

My dad stumbles in from the other bedroom in his underwear and a shiny blue hiking shirt and kneels by the bed. After fifteen minutes of forceful cajoling, he manages to wrest her legs from under her and swivel her onto the smooth orange sheets. It looks like she's fallen out of space, that mask strapped to her face like an astronaut's, her body smashed down.

I walk slowly back up the stairs and lie far away from Don. I try to close my eyes, but sleep won't come. I get up and pick some clothes up off the floor, careful not to say a single word, afraid of what will come out if I do. And hours later, Don is asleep and it shoots through me. The Bad Feeling.

"Where're you going?" Don asks, propping himself up on an elbow. Downstairs, in the bedroom, I see my father holding my mother upright. He's dazed; it takes him a minute to see me.

"What's going on?" I ask. I'm afraid to ask. It seems every day I look at him wincing, my hair pricking back off my scalp and I ask this. And every day he answers with a weary, "Oh, she just can't breathe," or "It's not a whole lot different," and the tiny guillotine above my heart loosens slightly and wedges its blade a little deeper. But he doesn't answer and I go to her side and I sit, all my muscles tight.

"The narcotics slowed her breathing," my dad says. His hands are on her pulse. "She took too many drugs, I think. She's dying."

And fire leaps through me. No. No. This isn't happening. I did it. I must have done it. It had something to do with that wad of pills. I must have administered the wrong one and now she's going to die from that, not from the cancer but from that. And she's turning purple on one side of her face, her head hanging over her chest like a broken flower.

And I realize now, in the dark room, that I am not ready, that I will never be ready, that her death will change me even though I've understood that it's been coming for nine years. And all the changes won't be hopeful—like the clarity of vision I sometimes feel when I'm in my bedroom after crying and the lines of the windows and slatted doors all look too sharp, hyper-sharp, and all people seem tragic and plain to me, easy to understand. Some of the changes will be only pain. Pain when I see babies, pain when my friends go to lunch with their mothers, pain on my birthday, on her birthday, on every birthday of every person I know. Pain and a deep, toothy hollowness inside me that will go on grinding forever.

"Mom, Open Your Eyes!" I yell. And I'm up off the bed, pacing. "What are we going to do?" I keep asking this. My dad counts her pulse. He watches her with that defeated awe I've grown used to, and he looks so tired, and I keep thinking it's got to be Barb's fault, shouldn't she have known this could happen? We got the drugs from her. My mom's liver is full of cancer, shouldn't she have realized we could poison her with this cocktail of narcotics? Did she slip Mom another pill, another patch? Why doesn't she ever warn us and where is she when we actually *need* her?

"Should we call hospice?" I ask. I am going to save my mother. I only know this. I only know I cannot lose her, not tonight, not yet. My dad says sure, sure, and I go find the lavender folder and bring it in. A nurse answers and I hand the phone to my dad.

"Well," he's saying, "my wife is comatose; she has respiratory failure and her respirations are slowing and she's going to stop breathing here if we don't get an injection to reverse the narcotics—" He pauses, listens.

And then the world stops, swings into reverse.

"No, it's true," he says, "she is a hospice patient, yes. Yes. It's true." And when he finally hangs up the phone we are not going to admit Mom to the ER, she's dying and we are going to allow it. We're going to give up Mom forever, hold her heavy head up so she doesn't go crashing into the metal of the railings of the bed next to her bed, and watch her die.

"She wouldn't want to go to the hospital, Robin," my dad says. And I can't really believe this—even though I know it's true—I can't believe that my mom wouldn't want to do whatever it took to stay living, to be my mother.

"Martha would want to be here for the end," my dad

says. I look at the clock. It's only ten at night, though it seems like it should be four in the morning, or a time that no one's ever heard of, a time that never existed before and I call Martha and through my sobs she understands and she comes, and Suzanne comes and they are trying to hold my mom's head up so she doesn't strangle; we are trying to keep her from keeling forward so she doesn't smack her head on the hospital bed railings. Martha wears tight black jeans and a ribbed orange shirt and she looks like she ought to be studying for something and Suzanne smells sweet, like hay. And they are bringing their hands around my mom's body, they are feeling for her energy field because once they tried to learn therapeutic touch and none of us is ready for this; I am willing her to come back, come back, and we are yelling: Take a Breath! Don't Stop! Open Your Eyes! Say My Name!

"Mom," I'm yelling, "Mom, can you hear me?" And I imagine her opening her eyes, that familiar love and irony coming right back in, and her smiling at me with those perfect white teeth.

"Yes, Ms. Melodrama," she'd say—a rocky tone to her voice. But she's barely breathing, nodding, keeling, she will not open her eyes. One breath, two breaths, and then none.

We try to force her backward onto the bed; we are tired, so tired, and we want her to lie down on her own. How can we spend the night like this, propping her up—it takes at least two people—but when we try to force her, her eyes fly open in alarm and she gasps *no*.

Don appears. Somewhere in all of this my father

goes into the kitchen and gets the tortilla chips and my dad and I sit there, hours and hours into the night, and we are eating chips and watching Mom while Martha and Suzanne hold her to keep her from falling. I can't look at Don. When I do, the whole thing feels like a performance. I can't explain this. She's choking, turning gray. We're all crying. We're willing God to come into the room and save her, save this woman he's done nothing but punish. And as the dark outside begins to soften back into light, my mother heaves a giant breath. Everyone pauses. And then, another. And then she seems to be breathing. It slowly begins to pick up and by dawn she's alive again.

Don's flight leaves early. We say very little to each other. What is there to say? "'Bye. I'll call you from the airport." I watch the high butt of the little rental car turn the corner down the hill and feel a strange vacancy.

A few hours later I realize I haven't heard from him, so I take out my cell phone. I press a few buttons and a dark square comes onto the screen, then woozily fades. My phone numbers are stored in here, and though I don't call anyone except for Don, I can't have it fail. Not now. Not when things are getting so bad. This little silver plastic box links me to California, my only bridge. I panic, load Mercy into the back of my car, and head down the hill to the cell phone store. I wait patiently in a tiny, air-conditioned room until the young woman behind the counter is free.

"I don't know what happened," I say sweetly. "It just stopped working." The woman looks like girls I went to high school with. Her nose appears to have little cartilage and at least three shades of blond stripe her hair. Against her starched T-shirt, the sleeves carefully cuffed, she wears a cross with tiny diamonds.

"You got it wet," Christina the cell phone representative says, handing the phone back to me. She's holding it like I urinated on it, with her index finger and thumb. My heart starts beating faster.

"I did not get it wet." I say this before thinking but after I say it, it becomes true. I did not get it wet! My entire body fills with indignation. Who is she to say I got it wet?

"Look," she says, pointing to a little box on the battery. This turns red if the phone gets wet. *And,*" she says, the side of her lip rising slightly, "see this little place where the plug goes?" She holds the base of the phone an inch from my face. I can see a small forest of turquoise dots growing in the finely grooved indentation. "It's rusting."

"I did not get the phone wet," I say. I feel tears and stave them off.

"You did get the phone wet." She types something into her computer. Her acrylic nails clack. "You have no insurance and now you'll have to buy a new phone. The cheapest one is around two hundred fifty dollars."

"The phone broke," I say. "It's not my fault."

"The phone got wet," she says.

"No it didn't. It just stopped working."

"You're not telling me the truth."

I am incredulous. "You're saying that I'm lying?" At this point, I have forgotten that I actually am lying. I have convinced myself that the phone is sick, that they can save the phone and yet they are choosing not to! I begin to shake from the inside and I can't breathe all the way in. I look calm, but my cheeks are tightening, my shoulders are knitted to my earlobes.

Christina raises her very plucked eyebrows. Her cross glitters cheaply.

"There's nothing I can do," she says. She likes this—there's a haughty, sadistic gleam in her eyes. A feeling I've not felt before creeps over me. I take the phone but I can't hold it. It falls to the counter. What is this feeling? As if I am face-to-face with God. I am having my moment. I can't let it pass.

"You," I say, leaning toward her. My voice is low and the words come slowly. "*Are a terrible person.* You could help me, *Christina,* but you're *choosing* not to."

Her eyes widen. She folds her arms across her chest, then lunges for the desk phone. She dials, then dangles the phone at me.

"Talk to headquarters," she says, spinning on her heels.

As soon as I start to tell my story to Elizabeth of headquarters, something gives inside me, as if all those tears were held back by cardboard that has finally soaked through. They have to save my phone! I know they can! I say this through sobs. My tears freak the woman out and she agrees to give me $100 off my new phone, plus a rebate, which will bring the phone down to $99. I hand the phone back to Christina so she can process it.

"The customer got this phone wet," I hear Christina

say. "You're going to authorize this even though the phone got wet?" She gives me a look, Barb's glare mixed with hate.

When I leave the store with my new phone, I have to sit down. I can't even get to my car. Perched on the orange curb, I wait as the tremors course through me.

In 1996, my mother had been ill only nine months when her mother, Florence, suffered respiratory failure. She battled, but in the end she fell into a coma. My mother's father, Norman, did not want a vegetable for a wife and he knew she would not have wanted it either. "I've loved that woman for sixty years," he said. "And I'm not wiping her when she goes to the bathroom." This was not the way they'd conceived of the end. My grandfather decided to unhook the respirator.

"I need you to go to Florida." My mother wept into the phone. I was in Rhode Island, trying to get schoolwork done despite the craziness of her diagnosis. I didn't understand why I had trouble focusing on my textbooks, why urban blight in Chicago didn't consume me the way it consumed my peers. It never occurred to me to blame the cancer, the news trickling in weekly— tumors, chemicals, percent chances of survival. I just figured I wasn't as smart as the other kids. I wanted to hang up on her, erase the newest development in the failing of the women in my family. I wanted to drink boxed wine in crappy dorm kitchens with my new friends. I wanted to go to bonfires under abandoned railroad bridges. But I also wanted to be entrusted with the weight of this. I was twenty years old, three thousand miles away, trying to bullshit my way through essays about postmodern theater techniques. My professors, famous and remote, spoke in a language that only the prep school kids understood. I struggled for my grades where I once got easy As and in the middle of it all, my mother wanted me to fly to Florida to say good-bye to her mother for her. She couldn't make the trip. Her doctors informed her that her radiation-chemo combo could not be interrupted again.

I flew to Miami and my uncle picked me up. We drove straight to the hospital, speaking little as we made our way down gray linoleum hallways to the small private room where my grandfather waited by her bedside. She looked smaller than I remembered. Her dark hair, threaded with gray, fell stiffly on the pillow. Her eyelids looked glued shut. A black transistor radio sang tinny, bouncy numbers about the longevity of true romance. My grandfather, dapper well into his seventies, wore a clean white T-shirt secured in his jeans with a belt. His lips seemed to move without his consent, though no words came out.

When I was much younger, maybe six, Norman, my grandfather, took me on a walk in Lincoln City, the silver Oregon ocean growling as the sun rose high over the dunes. He thought his thoughts, which he mostly kept to himself, and I studied the way the rocks were set into the path. Wind bent dune grass until it flattened into silver matting over the sand. Without warning, a seagull shot from the sky and shit on my shoulder. I wore my bright red Windbreaker, my only and favorite coat. "Oh no!" I said, looking cautiously at the sky. My grandfather took out his special hankie—the one with masculine boxes of gray. He shook his head and narrowed his eyes as he slid the cloth over the nylon.

"I must really love you," he said, shaking out his hankie before folding it back into his pocket. "That was my best rag."

And once, on another visit, my grandfather whispered that I was his favorite and it has always been there between us, a tiny bird humming its wings. We both know that the world holds unmentionable, unfathomable sorrow. We understand the understanding between us—the depth of the world and our place in it—and so speak brightly of tomato plants and dogs.

But that day he straightened the sheet of the adjustable hospital bed, over and over, yanking it to a military crispness over my grandmother's body. My uncle said, in his thick Brooklyn accent, "Robin is here, Mom. She's come to visit." My grandmother had been unconscious for days, unmoving. And they'd just taken her off the respirator. But at the mention of my name she grew agitated and her eyes began to flutter.

"Florence!" my grandfather pleaded. His grip on her hand tightened and she appeared to be there, fighting just below her deeply tanned and wrinkled skin. The whites of her eyes flickered and then the lids closed again. She'd made a near recovery a week before. My grandfather, in a fit of grief, had taken all of her earthly possessions—clothes and shoes, books and paints, and bagged them into trash bags, set them on the curb. My mother, horrified, asked him what he was going to do if my grandmother lived. When she woke up, he'd have to admit that he'd rid himself of every trace of her. And when it looked, briefly, like this could be the case, he seemed to grow taller, new threads of green landed in his eyes and he said if she woke up, he would buy her all new things, everything and anything she wanted, more than she'd ever dreamed of having!

We sat there for a while, staring at her, until my uncle suggested we get some sodas from the vending machine. We slid our dollars in and waited for the clank of our change, the thud of the bottle.

But when we got back to the room, a nurse was adjusting some charts on the table by my grandmother's bed. She looked uncomfortable, caught.

"She's passed," the nurse said, averting her eyes. And she left us there, standing stupidly with our sodas, the radio asking *Won't you, won't you, won't you be my girl?* My grandfather walked to the side of the bed, his head bent. "The lady always has to have the last word," he said dryly, the tears in his throat held back by something strong and hard inside him.

My grandfather turned away, his back to us. My uncle looked to the ceiling and put his hands on my shoulders. But I stared at the skin on her face. I wanted to see if it would tell me something. She'd turned a new color in the few minutes since she'd died, a yellowy gray. Nothing about her moved. I leaned forward but my uncle directed me toward the door.

"Let's go, Dad. Let's go."

Back at their apartment, my uncle got out a case of Corona and we sliced lime and sat at the kitchen table in front of the mirrored wall. I had just started seeing a boy in college—very good looking, though very remote. I called to tell him and he said little, murmured condolences, and I pretended that he had said something comforting. I dreamed that night of my grandmother's body coming to pieces, the bones revealing themselves, the yellow skin peeling back. I sat up in bed, the little neon numbers of the clock casting a green glow on the sofa bed, and thought I felt something, a ghost, a message, but I couldn't put words to it.

When we told my mother, she cried and cried. "But I need her! I'm not well!" She wept on airplanes and in restaurants. And when she did this, I would lock my heart. I refused to touch her. I could not allow her the indulgence. You cannot lose the people that you love when you most need them; this did not happen, could not happen. In order to beat death, you couldn't admit to being vulnerable to it.

I believed this thoroughly and in the ninth year, I went to see a psychoanalyst who made me speak of my fear of my mother dying. A month after this, my mother got the news that there was nothing left to try. That the tumors were everywhere. That she would die.

My mother used to say to me, "It's terrible to lose your mother at the end of your life. You don't know what it's like." This always struck me as a bizarre one-upmanship. My loss, according to this logic, would be obfuscated by jobs and babies and walks in spring to feed the geese. According to my mother, my hurt would fade. It would not, as I claimed, be pain I carried for years. *Her* loss would expand. The loss of her mother would simply get larger and larger as it ushered her into her own death. Her mother's death was not a loss to be obscured by joys. It was an introduction of sorts: This is what it looks like, baby. Hold on to your wig.

Mom swims in and out of sense. She hasn't recovered from that horrible night. She won't recover. The plethora of meds, the respiratory failure—these things have conspired against her brain, have addled and damaged it. I can't get my own brain to register the truth of it. I don't understand the body, I've decided. And I'm beginning to realize that her words, her gestures, her thoughts and ideas—these are bodily, too.

The morning after the overdose, my father and I sat next to each other at the kitchen table. "This is terrible," he said. Again, he looked so fragile, so afraid, his hair mussed and his arms thin.

"I think we shouldn't medicate her anymore," I say. "I think we should only give her the anxiety pills and the pain meds if she's anxious or in pain." My father nods. I imagine Barb's vinyl bag, that bag which sometimes appears larger than life, a bag we could crawl into, wandering down aisles of pills, down carpets of gauze. A bag filled with the muffled sound of questions that can't get asked, of love that cannot be expressed, of memories shut off by chemicals. We agree, my dad and I. When our eyes meet I feel a swirl of intensity. My father and I are tied by blood and love to this woman, to this house, to this problem that keeps metastasizing and will metastasize, we know, until it shatters.

♦ ♦ ♦

I'm on one of the wooden chairs in the kitchen, knitting. The dark brown wool has white spun into it and Mom's watching me from her wheelchair.

"Do you like it?" I ask. It's ugly. It's supposed to be a scarf for Don's birthday, but it looks like a throw rug. My mom nods.

"What's it made of?" she asks, trying to hold her head steady.

"Wool," I say. "Yarn."

"I KNOW," she says, like I'm a moron. "But what's in it?"

"Wool," I say. "It's brown with white in it."

"I KNOW, but garlic. Isn't that garlic?" I look at the white yarn threaded through the dark and it's true, in a way. It does sort of look like garlic.

Later, she turned to Melinda, her best friend from law school who's visiting from her cattle farm near Walla Walla and she asked: *What have we done that's ironic?* Melinda stopped wiping my mom's face with the washcloth and she said, "Oh Jackie, everything." Melinda's been wandering around the hallways all day, repeating this.

On very bad days, Mom will look up at me, fear and pain staining the brown in her eyes, and she will say, "I want to go home."

"You are home, Mom," I say, holding her hand, which is hard as plastic from edema.

"I know," she says, her face pleading, "but I want to go *home*." My dad says I'm attaching meaning to this when it's nonsense.

♦ ♦ ♦

Mercy won't quit chasing Lily. Every time she sees the kitten, or the tail of the kitten, or the kitten's shadow, a bolt of electricity shoots through her. Lily seems to want this abuse. She'll sense the dog and slow down, prancing right across Mercy's line of vision until a low, vicious growl bursts from my submissive, groveling dog and they're off, charging around the house, their small bodies tilted sideways. Then Lily soars up, stretching through the air, and lands effortlessly on the counter. Mercy, when reprimanded for this, looks terrorized, tucking her tail and slinking under chairs. I'd reprimand Lily, too, but I can't figure out how to talk to a cat.

In fact, last night, when I teetered on the edge of sleep, Lily found her way into my bedroom. She found a bobby pin on the dresser and, because she is smart and dexterous, launched this pin into a ceramic vase. I didn't want to get up, but the clinking wouldn't quit. Obsessively, she stirred this pin around, catching it on her claw and dropping it. When I finally grabbed her and told her to stoppit, she yowled in protest, pitiful yowls that pierced me to my core.

I'm so tired of negotiating animals. Right now I have Mercy by her collar, holding her with one hand while eating one of my mom's Popsicles with the other. The sky is darkening early these days. A navy light falls toward the trees. Melinda finds me. She crosses her arms and widens her stance, like a cowgirl.

"Has that dog been out?" she asks. I let Mercy go and she runs to Melinda, sits cockeyed on one hip, and stares at Melinda's fingers, willing them to come closer. I shake my head.

"I think we should take her to the dog park," she says.

"Is it open at night?"

"Let's find out," she says.

The gate at the dog park, it turns out, has no lock. Tall streetlamps send light down to the grass, illuminating the filthy water of the kiddie pools. Mercy seems disinterested in exercise. She smells something near a pool and gets lodged beside it. I toss a ball and it lands somewhere in the dark field.

"How are things going with Don?" she asks. Melinda's one of my mom's oldest friends. The two of them also pulled late nights on the sofa, laughing, comparing notes on work and marriage. I remember being so small, sitting on the sofa in our old house, peering out the window to the front walkway. Melinda, her arms full of books, came up to the door, her long braid swinging over the butt of her tight jeans. She saw me in the window and made a scary face, scrunching up her skin and sticking out her tongue. My heart beat in fear. And now, twenty-six years later, concern draws her features toward each other in a different sort of scrunching. She says that when her mother was dying, she knew she'd married the right man. She says some things to me about love and trust. I can't answer her question. If I say how angry I am, no one will understand what it is that Don offers me every night on the phone, how he does try to listen to me, even if he fumbles often with his responses. Even if he doesn't know what to say.

Fourth of July weekend, when I was staying in Eugene, Don and I arranged to unite for a weekend in

Ashland, a small tourist town near the California border. The second night there, we found an old steak house with a kitschy sign and red vinyl booths. We grinned at each other over baskets of garlic bread, then took our blanket to the hills and watched a faltering, poorly organized fireworks display. The next day we found out about swimming holes along the Applegate River. We got too late a start, though, and by the time we found the pools the trees cast dark shadows over the current. I dared him to swim and he dared me and we stripped down and shrieked, calling each other wimps as our skin hit the freezing river.

And before all of this, for his birthday a year or two ago, I brought a mix CD to his small studio in San Francisco—the one that reeked of mildew from the carpeted bathroom—and we had a dance party, just Don and I, prancing in teeny tiny circles in the cramped space. We got so focused on our moves that we never went out for dinner as we'd planned. We kept going, waving our arms in the air, painting the wall with our booties, until we collapsed in a fit of exhaustion.

"I don't know," I say to Melinda. "I don't know what I feel." I walk into the field to find the ball. I can't talk, can't answer. I'm so afraid that the truth might be this: I can't deal with love anymore. Not after this.

The next day, someone straightens up the counter and finds the ballot. It's time to vote. Oregon has shifted to mail-in ballots and this year it's the presidential election: George Bush versus John Kerry. My mother has always been political, cajoling me to speak at rallies, to be on student government, to make myself heard. Because of her, I've worked in sex education, the prison system, a camp for children affected by HIV. I've investigated civil rights complaints in sweatshops in Saipan. I've written letters to senators, read case law just for fun. In September, when I came here, I didn't think to arrange for a California absentee ballot and now I feel panicky, like a bad citizen, someone my mother would shake her head at. A lazy, selfish person that God might refuse to help. I call and have an absentee ballot FedExed to me. It costs a fortune and I have to turn around and FedEx it back.

"It's voting time," my father says. My mother leans to one side in her wheelchair at the kitchen table. Her collection of folk dolls from all the countries she's been to hovers on a shelf above her head. I'm struck by the creepiness of a doll from Budapest—a doll with a dried apple for a head. When we bought the doll, the face had been whitish, but it wasn't preserved properly and now, though the doll has peach-colored hands, her face has turned a purple-black. My mother's head slumps and her eyes are flat. I watch her try to gather her wits. She's still far away, in the land where wool is garlic.

"Do you want to check the ballot?" my father asks, dangling the pen in front of her. She sits still. She blinks. He waits, and when she doesn't move, he checks the boxes he knows she'd want marked. "It's the presidential election, Jackie," he says. My mother hates George Bush's policies on the war, social services, the arts. She also hates people who fail to vote and then complain about the way the world works. She has never missed a chance to vote. "Here, sign it," he says. Her arm shakes so hard that when she takes the pen from him, she can't hold on to it. She lets it drop to the floor as if it burned her fingers. My father picks it up, puts it into her hand. She presses it to the ballot and draws a wild-looking zigzag for a signature. Gone is the slanted, sensual penmanship of her many years on earth. This is the scrawling of a toddler. My mom gestures to the bedroom.

My father carries the ballot to the counter, then back to the kitchen table, then over the sofa under the light. He studies the scrawl, changing the angle of the ballot to see if it makes a difference. "If they have anything to compare this to, it'll be tossed out as a fraud," my father says. He cannot put the ballot down. He appears to be willing the signature to revert back to what it ought to look like, what it would have looked like before that awful, overmedicated night. "This is horrible," he says, staring out at the trees. I think of my mother in her silk blouses, her eyelashes curled, her amethyst earrings sparkling. When, eight years ago, old colleagues of hers from a previous firm failed to say anything when she was diagnosed with cancer, but instead called to say she owed them money, my mother simmered with rage. "I'm going to get fancy stationery," she said. "And across the top I'm going to emboss in gold: Fuck Off."

"It has to count," my father says to the ballot. "It's her last vote."

I don't want my mother to die. She's downstairs now, her breathing labored, her face creased and ashen. She's swollen everywhere and on her sternum you can actually see the skin puffed out where the tumors have grown, like a basketball rising from her chest. Barb can't understand why my mother continues to go on, why she doesn't take more medicine to make herself "comfortable."

"I don't understand why she continues to suffer." Barb has me cornered by the red double doors that lead out to the wet Oregon night. She's straightening up her files. "I think she's holding on for you." Her blue eyes are glittery and cool. She begins to wind her purple scarf around her neck. "You need to tell her that she can die, that you'll be okay."

This is not the first time someone has told me this. That someone has suggested that if I dig into my pockets I will find a little brass key that will unlock the door to a happy, peaceful death.

But no matter how many times someone tells me a story about "releasing the dying," I'm not going to say this. I won't be okay. And this is not only because her movements and thought patterns are my own, not because I have talked to her almost every day of my life—but because "okay" is a dumb word.

I will not be okay. It would be like being nice. I may be anguished and exhausted or anxious and excited or full of buzzing. But I am never okay. And when my mom dies it will be crushing pain, a silence that will fill me and break me over and over again, daily, relentlessly. The idea of losing her has been careening around me since I was nineteen like a maniac bird and I'm not stupid, I've paid attention. There is nothing okay about it.

"I can't do that," I say to Barb, and I'm crying—it's sudden, my throat hurts. My eyes are hot.

"She's suffering," Barb says. "Can't you do it for her? It would be your final present."

"I don't want her to die."

"But her spirit will always live in you," Barb says.

"I don't believe in that," I say.

"What? Spirit?" Barb asks. I nod. She shakes her head and takes a step toward the door. "Well, I do, I truly do," she says. The darts in her gaze have melted and now she is pitying, now she is on a tall boulder looking down. "I suppose, in a way it makes it easier for me." And I think that this is true—and I'm jealous of people with heaven, but I can't believe any of that after nine years of her suffering. There is no order to the universe and I can't sign up for one.

And right before she shuts herself safely out of this death house, she looks straight at my face as if she must articulate this in order to believe it. "You are a sweet being, Robin." She shakes her head. And then she's gone.

Barb left me two brochures by the kitchen phone. One is the customary lavender. In gothic font over a Xeroxed tree it reads, "Caring for a Family Member Approaching Death." I open the book to the first page: blank. A promising sign. That's how the book should look. Twelve blank pages. But then, I turn to the next. It says:

The experience we call death occurs when the body completes the physical process of shutting down and the spirit releases from the body, it's [sic] imme-diate environment, and all attachments. Physically, this is an orderly and undramatic [sic] series of bodily changes which do not require emergency medical attention.

There are several lists of symptoms and a little para-graph about "giving permission to let go."

It may be helpful to lay [sic] in bed with your loved one and then say everything you need to say. It may be as simple as saying "I love you". Tears are a normal and natural part of saying "Good-Bye". Tears do not need to be hidden from your loved one or apologized for. Tears express your love and help you let go.

I shut the booklet and rip it in half. The other brochure is entitled, "The Power of Prayer." I don't bother to look at that one. Barb, after carefully acknowl-edging my Jewish ancestry, mentioned that it included a Web URL for purchasing a prayer that would be put into the Jerusalem wall. I shove the papers under other papers and go upstairs.

I take pills to go to sleep. I swim out into a blank world, full of heaviness and white. I stumble downstairs for coffee when I wake up—the sun is torturously bright through the skylights. I'm still gooey from the drugs, and suddenly I feel it—a rage so intense I can't hold my cof-fee cup. Who does Barb think she is? What is this busi-ness about suffering? Barb started coming here two weeks ago, but this has been going on nine years. My mother has suffered long and hard to stay in the world. If there hadn't been suffering, there wouldn't have been life. And why should she give up today? Tonight? Why should she look out the windows at the large fir trees, the blue sky turning bright with impending winter, the dogs panting at the glass door—why should she see the beautiful cherrywood dresser she chose a year ago, the whimsical paintings of bulbous-headed girls on bicycles, the photographs of me with my graduation cap on, the books she's been meaning to read, the lists of people who've called her—why should she see all the pieces of her world and wish to leave it?

My dad comes to the table and says, "You should get dressed. The social worker is coming."

"Why didn't you tell me?" I yell. I hate him! And I hate The Social Worker, though she's new to us (our old one had to deal with a personal crisis and quit her job)—I don't want any more people coming in to this house with their maps to heaven, telling us our time is up, that Mom is better off obliterated, better as a heap of rotting cells in a plain pine box.

"Tell her not to come," I say.

"Robin," my dad says.

"Fine!" I shove the chair away. My whole face stretches. My eyes bulge. Suzanne and Martha walk into the kitchen. I hate them, too. I'd trade every single one of them for another week with my mother.

I run upstairs and get dressed. I have no idea what I'm wearing. A shirt. Pants. Socks. Green, red, black, brown—things to cover the body. I take a clip and ball my hair into it. If I look crazy, all the better. I hate them all. I won't bathe, I won't brush my teeth. I don't want anyone near me, not now, not ever.

The bell rings. My dad's gone outside with the dogs and in the bathroom, Martha and Suzanne are giving my mother a sponge bath. I take a deep breath and go to the door.

"I'm Dora," the woman says. I'm speechless. She extends her hand to me but I can't take it.

"*You're* The Social Worker?" My lip is curling. "You're my age!"

This woman can't know anything, she's no older than twenty-six. I gape at her outstretched hand. My dad walks in through the back door and strides quickly toward us. He's afraid of me. At times like this I become my mother—formidable and razor-tongued.

"I'm Richard," he says. Dora shakes his hand. She wears an orange hand-knitted scarf and a tan corduroy jacket. A mess of papers sticks out from the corner of a messenger bag.

"I can't deal with this." I rush past them. I take the front door in my hands and throw it back, so hard that when it slams, the entire house seems to wobble and the dying pink fuchsia that my mom paid such careful attention to every year of my life swings on its little wire hook. I don't have shoes on. I run down the cold wooden steps in my socks. The day is Oregon fall—crisp, some wetness on the pavement from the early-morning fog and dew. I am half running, half walking down the hill, through this quiet wooded neighborhood, the same route I used to walk when I went trick-or-treating twenty years ago. I go down down down the hills, the autumn sun mixing with the cold air, warming my dark hair—and then I have to go up. It's hard work, this hiking in socks, and it's both a relief and an embarrassment that nobody's following me.

But where am I going? It's been ten years since I lived here and I don't know anyone. There's no secret fort behind the house anymore, there are no boys to lure out of carpeted dens to thrash out new trails through the brambles. And anyway, the forests behind the houses have mostly been developed. What used to be woods are now brightly lit track homes with immaculately landscaped yards.

I huff my way up the hill. I haven't worked this hard in ages and spikes stab my lungs. It's starting to hurt. I force myself past this. I have half a mind to keep on going, to walk forever and not stop, to wear a hole in my socks, sleep in the soft mud beneath porches, wash with leaves, go far enough away that I can no longer remember who I am or where I came from. But I also know I'm turning down the street that will lead me back to our cul-de-sac, back to that death house, its red door.

I can hear them talking in the living room. I can't bear it. I go into my mom's bedroom. She's alone and awake, her BiPAP humming. She looks at me.

"Mom," I say. And I start crying—hot tears of fury.

"Whus sss," she says, holding out a swollen arm. I go toward her and kneel on the floor so that my head is level with hers. She strokes my hair.

"I want them all to go away," I sob. "Get them to go away." She continues to pet my head. "I hate them.

106

They're not helping. They don't know us, they just want to kill you and I don't want you to die."

My mother stops petting me and she says, through the mask, "Bring them in here." I'm suddenly ashamed. Is she going to try and rally? What's she going to say?

"No, Mom," I say.

"Bring them in here," she repeats.

"No." She takes her hand back and stares at me. I'm racing to get a grip, breathing my tears in. "Fine." I laugh nervously and wipe my eyes.

"Dad," I say. He's sitting with Dora, Martha, and Suzanne. I can't look at any of them. "Mom wants to talk to you."

He follows me back into the bedroom. My mom gives me an exasperated look.

"She wants to talk to everyone," I say.

"Well, go get them," my dad says.

I don't want to see those women. I want to be remembered as the girl who slammed the red door, not the girl whose dying mother had to advocate for her. But I go into the living room and ask them to come in. Dora and my father sit on the bed with my mother. Suzanne, Martha, and I sit on the hospital bed.

"Hi, Jackie," Dora says. She has an interesting accent. Polish? I hate her.

My mom blinks her purple lids.

"Robin's." She pauses. "Upset." It wears her out to do this, to talk on my behalf. It's amazing that she even can. Much of the day, she can't call soup by its correct name, can't form words for the pain of the mask. This is humiliating.

I look at Dora. "I'm sorry," I say. "But I don't like your hospice thing at all. You walk into a house you don't know, into a family who's been living next to death for years and years, and you tell us what to think of it. How dare you. You tell us what our grief should look like, what we'll feel, and how to let go. You tell us about spirit as if you know, as if you have any idea what will happen to the person who's dying. Fuck you, fuck all of you. This isn't your family and who do you think you are? God? Saints? Angels of death? I don't like being talked down to—I haven't liked Barb and honestly, I have no intention of liking you."

I'm shaking, but I feel lighter. Dora looks like she swallowed a dry piece of rope. She fingers her folder.

"You're right," she says. "I don't know you. And I'm sorry if hospice has come across in the way you describe. This is not my family, though I have enjoyed meeting your mother. She seems like a wonderful woman—this is not my family and there's no way I could do my job if it was. It would be too hard. I don't know what you are going through. Only you know that. And I'm sorry. This is the hardest thing."

I look at Dora sideways. She's pretty. Wisps of honey-colored hair have fallen out of her French braid and she's got on dark, owlish glasses.

"And by the way," she says, "I'm thirty-six."

It's October. Soon it will be Halloween. Outside there are pumpkins and dry corn and little skeletons hanging in windows. I let Mercy off her leash at the dog park and she runs quickly away from me, skidding to the side whenever large dogs approach. She's frightened of everything, her little ears tucked down. I'm scared, too.

But mostly I feel ragged. Hospice seems to me to be the same thing as assisted suicide, without protocol or consent. Nurse-inflicted homicide. Barb comes with enough morphine to kill, a tight schedule, and an unspoken agenda. She doesn't ask anyone when she slips Mom a pill. And one of these days, Barb's generosity with meds will speed us to the end. Is it how terrible my mom looks that makes killing her so necessary? She's not crying out in pain; she's uncomfortable, but she's been uncomfortable for years. And these years have been full of talks on the sofa and walks with the dogs, sandwiches, cupcakes, and stories. Barb argues that the drugs are humane, as if my mom's a horse or fallen bird. But shouldn't my mom ask for the meds? Shouldn't my mom be the one begging to die? And if she's too out of it some days to know what's in the glass she's drinking or why there are tubes in her nose, why does Barb get to make the decision to up the fentanyl, the morphine? What gives Barb the right to decide when Mom's no longer meant for this world?

Before I arrived back here a few weeks ago, my mom sat my dad down and told him she was interested in learning about doctor-assisted suicide. She asked if, when the time came, he would administer her the drugs. My father said no, he just couldn't. She could do what she wanted, but he couldn't be involved. He asked me if I thought I would be capable of that—a few days ago when things felt so bad we couldn't go on, when it seemed like we might all die before she did. But I'm not a boat builder, none of us is.

And Mom keeps on holding out. Is it just her body, so accustomed to fighting? Is it habit, after nine years, to overcome breathlessness and extraordinary pain? Is it love for me that keeps her here, as my dad and Barb say? Or love of color and texture and taste and smell and the hope of seeing the ocean one last time? Or is it that she's still young, her body is tough, her will is strong, and she just can't die yet?

It's evening and my fury has settled into something more disturbing. I go to my mother to see if she needs anything, a milkshake, a bowl of soup. But I don't even ask her. I climb next to her in the bed.

I feel I owe her some explanation for the episode with the social worker, though she would never demand that of me, being a person who would have done exactly the same thing.

I tell my mom what Barb said to me.

"I know it's selfish," I say. "But I can't tell you it's okay to die. I won't be okay." My words are coming too fast. "I'll try to go on, I'll try to live a life you'd be proud of, but I can't imagine life without you and I can't tell you to die."

My mom stares at me with her wide brown eyes. She looks at people these days in the same way she looks at the clock by her bed or the television on the dresser or the large wall-length crack in her wall.

It's hard to hear her through the whirring of the BiPAP mask.

"Thank you, sweetie," she says. "I dun want to die. But at thiz point, iss what should happen." Tears stream down my cheeks. I'm getting the pillows damp. "And, sweetheart, I dun need your permission."

This is what I wanted to hear; it's my release.

I repeat this to my dad in the kitchen. He's drinking expensive wine and eating a banana. He shakes his head. The way things have been the past couple of days, it's hard to believe she could rally to have this conversation. And he says, bitterly, "Your mom would come out of a coma if you said you needed her."

I go to bed hopeful that somehow I'll be able to keep her afloat, even though we're losing ground every day, even though yesterday a lesion opened on her leg and fluid from the swelling began oozing quickly out, drenching the sheets, the rug—I'll remain true to the mission we signed up for nine years ago: more life, at any cost.

The day that started this last round of dying, a couple of weeks ago, is written in my journal, the only entry I have made in a journal, the only entry I will make. The pen's too slow, the pages too square.

October 6, 2004

Today's the day Mom decided to go off chemo. Her breast was crimson, blue, purple and puckered like rotting fruit. The nipple was barely visible.

It's incredible and terrifying to think that she is here now and soon she will be gone. I can not wrap my head around this and I feel so alone.

*I took a valium. The world is dark. I feel shad-
ows nipping at my heels. Each day is a threat.*

I wrote this after our visit to the local oncologist,
maybe a week and a half after I arrived. We wheeled
Mom to the elevator, then into that little off-white room.
My dad and I sat on hard plastic chairs and waited for
Dr. Kovaks. He breezed in with his folders, looking
impervious, his beard so manicured it made me wonder
what his sock drawer looked like. He perched lightly on
his stool, as if he might need to spring up and out of the
room any second and didn't want to get too comfortable.

The scans had shown a marked increase in the
tumor mass. It bloomed in her liver, dark spots against
gray matter. And the tumor near her lungs was getting
so big it was cutting off her airways.

I can't remember the specifics of the conversation,
only that at some point my mom looked at the doctor
and asked to speak to her family in private. And when
he left the room, bouncing off his little stool gratefully,
she turned to me.

"I'm not going to do any more treatments, Robin."
In her eyes fear sparked, so hot and alive I couldn't
look back at her. "I can't do this anymore. I can't walk,
I can't breathe. I just can't live like this." She reached for
my hand, but I didn't want to touch her. How could she
do this to me? How could she choose to let the cancer
win? She took my hand anyway.

"It's your decision, Jackie," my dad said, leaning
over to kiss her cheek. "We love you. And we're sad but
we understand."

But it wasn't true. I didn't understand. The pain, the intensity of that discomfort, the feeling for years that you're suffocating. I only understood the fight against this, not the thing itself, not its ultimate victory.

"I'm sorry, sweetheart," my mom said, starting to cry.

I said nothing to her for the rest of the day. She told the doctor what she'd decided and he nodded and in his most efficient manner said, "I think you're making the right choice, Jackie. Any treatments we tried at this point might just make you feel worse and they'd have a minimal chance of changing the direction of the tumors. This way you can feel better for a while and enjoy the time you have left." He'd already announced that that would be anywhere from two months to a year. Then he told us if we were going to do this, we ought to sign up for hospice. He handed us a few sheets of paper and then patted me on the back before he walked out. "Hang in there, kiddo," he said.

I didn't stop shaking all day. I shook and cried and felt sick.

"Are you angry with me?" my mom asked. And I nodded but I couldn't speak. And she got into bed and she lay like stone and I came in and lay next to her, crying and crying as if my tears would change her mind, give her the strength for one more fight. But she got more and more still and more and more silent and finally she closed her eyes and I understood that it was all symbolic at this point. My gestures made in the face of a terrible void.

♦ ♦ ♦

I haven't been able to call my friends. I don't know what to say. "Hi, Robin," they say into my voice mail. "Just calling to see how you're doing" or "Just calling to see how you are" or "Just calling to see what you're up to." And all my answers to these questions seem morose and hyperbolic. I'm horrible, I'm blank, I'm drowning. I'm aging so fast. In December, instead of twenty-nine I will turn fifty-eight. Death is as available as tuna fish, as milk. It hovers next to me all the time but I can't see it. I feel it, though, its cold fingers tapping on my neck. And who has time to call friends? I don't know where the hours go, but emergencies surface hourly—a tube's come loose, a bandage needs changing, Ellen wants signatures on the retirement money allocation forms, the dog needs a walk, or I am just so tired, so tired it's like all the fluid has been sucked out of me, then blasted back in by great force, and all I can do is lie there while my body responds.

And in the past, when I've tried to answer—like when a professor in graduate school noticed me tearing up in class and asked me if I was okay—I get the weirdest responses. When I told the professor that my mom was dying, she looked at me. "I feel for you. My dog's dying," she said. It's better not to say anything, I thought. Better to just live with the distance between myself and the rest of the world.

But the calls from Camas I answer. We've been friends for thirteen years. I tell her, "If you want to see my mom one last time, you should come."

I pick her up at the airport with Mercy in the back of the car. It's strange to see her. I'm not sure what to say.

I have no way of telling all the dying concisely. We drop her bags off at a friend of her family's where she'll stay most nights, and then walk Mercy to the dog park.

Camas doesn't really like dogs, and Mercy's acting like a lunatic, jumping all over people and barking. There's rain on the grass, and the green turns silver in certain light. We walk, side by side, on the wet beige gravel, around the top half of the large two-tiered dog park, then through the battered gate and around the perimeter of the lower half. We breathe in the scent of our pasts, sitting in various parks after classes let out— the richness of mud and green plants, a faraway mineral smell from the rain. Trees shudder. One car swooshes by on the road outside the gate, sending a puddle of water up into the air. Across the park, a golden Lab crouches in front of a ball and rolls it with his nose. Mercy runs halfway across the park toward the dog, freezes, and barks. She turns to me as if for guidance. I pick up a stick and toss it halfheartedly.

A distance hums between Camas and me. I feel dumpy and tired in my jeans and sweater. She's just off a plane from New York, her hair clipped out of her face. She wears soft fitted pants. Her brown cardigan brings out the dark in her blondish hair. She's always been very tall and very thin and she walks across the wet grass with trepidation. She tells me about an annoying lady on the plane. I say very little about my life. I mention Don, our phone calls. I apologize when Mercy charges her and jumps against her hips.

After the park we drive around town, both of us gazing at the cheaply built houses sitting beneath giant firs, the natural food stores where we used to buy our salads and yogurt, the parks where we made out with boys. When we arrive back at the house, my mom is sleeping. Another couple has brought dinner. Baking dishes sit on the counter, covered with plastic wrap. The food looks like hay in the throes of decomposition. "It's vegan Chinese," my dad says. We set the table and put the food in the oven. Camas starts to relax. We sit around the wooden table and fill wineglasses. "Have you been to the Saturday Market?" she asks. I shake my head. We decide to go tomorrow, both of us eager for the noodles you have to wait on line for—slick with a fatty peanut sauce. I decide that if we go, I'll buy some hand-cut oatmeal soap for the bathroom upstairs. If it weren't for my father hovering over us and tubes coiled by the phone, it could be ten years ago. Maybe Camas and I will go upstairs and lie on our backs and strain to see stars out of my tree-blocked bedroom window. Maybe we will burn Nag Champa incense and dig through the old vintage dresses still hanging in my closet. We'll layer them over tattered jeans and put on dried rose tiaras and discuss spells and boys and whether or not there is life beyond this one.

When my dad finally wheels my mother to the table, she looks terrible—her face creased from the pillows and tubing. Her hair hangs in greasy clumps. The gray polyester bathrobe I bought her at Target falls open and you can see the disfigured breast beneath the pale nightgown. A moment passes before Camas can speak. She presses her hands into the table.

"Hi, Jackie!" she says, cheerful.

My mom smiles with her entire being. Her face, her eyes—she even lifts her hands slightly.

"Hi, Camas," she falters. "It's nice to see you."

"It's so good to see you, too," Camas says.

"I'm sorry . . . I look . . . so terrible," my mother says.

"Oh no," Camas says. "Not at all! I'm just really happy to get a chance to visit."

My mom smiles wryly and jerks to one side. "So . . . diplomatic," she says.

We can't eat the stranger's food. We never can. We push oily strands around our plates in little designs and I remember a painting that Camas made in high school of a man standing under an umbrella. It was a really good painting; she excelled in all aesthetic pursuits, and I glance over to see if she's made anything nice out of her greasy vegan stir-fry.

"I'll heat some tomato soup. Who wants some?" I ask. But no one does. The world outside is dark. The halogen light gleams in the corner. Camas gets up, gathers some dishes, and goes into the kitchen to cry.

My grandfather has just been released from the hospital for the second time. He's sitting at his kitchen table in the small carpeted apartment he rents at Willamette Oaks Retirement Center. The carpets once were white but God knows what he spilled all over the place. The hall that runs from the door to the small kitchen is stained a murky gray.

Camas tries to sit on the couch, but the zigzag upholstery is covered in months of *The New York*

Times. She starts to stack some on the mirrored coffee table.

"Tell her to stop that!" my grandfather yelps. He gets riled when people mess with his stuff. That's why no one can get in to clean this place. Wadded napkins have fallen, large snow, all over the surfaces. His place mats, relics from when vinyl had just emerged on the scene, are streaked brown with age.

"Sit here." I motion to the chair next to my grandfather. Camas comes and sits, crosses her long legs.

"Oh," my grandfather moans. He's wan and frail, his thin hair combed over his scalp. There's a close, deep odor in the room. Oranges and metal and something rank. He shakes his head as if there's water in his ear.

"You doing okay?" I ask. Every time something spikes with my mom, my grandfather seems to collapse. We've been running him in and out of the hospital for two weeks. Two days ago I visited him in the small beige hospital room, just across the street from the oncology office. He was lying in the adjustable bed, his arms strapped to an IV bag. With only a soft blue nightie on, he looked so fragile. His eyelids were a strange, plasticky white.

"Hello, Robin," he said. With his heavy Brooklyn accent, my name has three syllables. He peered at me, making no move toward vitality. He slowly lifted his tiny arm and then let it fall dramatically back on the bed.

"How's your father?" he asked.

"No one's doing very well," I said.

"God," he cried, "now this! A real doubleheader!"

118

"How're you feeling?" I asked. He took a sip of something milky and grimaced.

"They're going to run some tests," he said. "But I can't do surgery! I won't go! Robin—there's money hidden in the apartment." I waited. When my father was moving him into his apartment here, he found five hundred dollars in a yogurt container in the freezer.

"Look in the books!" he started. Without his dentures, his lips caved slightly. "In the Russian essayists. And also under the hutch—the one on the left. And in the baby shoes—do you know where they are?" I shook my head. "Oh! You have to look! You have to be so careful! In the shoe shine kit. And in the sugar bowl. I put cuff links in one of the vitamin bottles. And also, a box of quarters in the back of the desk. You have to move the desk. Check the mattress, too. Underneath."

"What about your coats?" I teased. My father recently went to get my grandfather's sport jacket cleaned and found an envelope full of fifty-dollar bills pinned to the lining.

"And take my library books back!"

"When are they due?" I asked. Why were we talking about this? How did he seduce me into worrying over a seventy-five-cent fine? He didn't answer.

"And Robin," he said, "cancel the *Times.*"

This was serious.

"You're not planning to make it through?" I asked.

"Oh!" he cried. "I need to use the bathroom!" He clutched the sheets.

"Here," I said, pressing the little remote, raising the head of the mattress. Here goes Grandpa, up up and away. He swiveled his legs out of the bed. They looked like little white sticks, almost hairless. Incredible, life—look how old it can get. He stood and moved toward the bathroom and I thought he looked pretty spry, for a dying ninety-one-year-old. And then an alarm began to ding.

"What is that?" I asked. I tried to get around the bed to grab my grandfather's arm but the nurses were already rushing in.

"What are you doing?" a bored one said. She wore gold jewelry and had bad skin.

"It's an EMERGENCY!" my grandfather screamed. "Get me to the toilet!"

Another nurse with a Betty Page hairdo began fiddling with the IV. "Just a minute," she said. She attempted to get the IV back in his arm. There was a problem with the clear tape.

"I DON'T HAVE A MINUTE!" my grandfather shrieked.

"Now, just a minute, Mr. Romm." But he tugged his tubes into the bathroom and they had to follow him. The older nurse dragged the IV stand and shut the door partway.

On a purple caregiver's guide beside the bed, I read: *Be kind to yourself! Take a moment a day to go outside. Remember to eat fruits and vegetables—your health is just as important!* I flipped it over and began to write down the various places my grandfather told me to hunt for money.

"Get your HANDS OFF ME!" His voice was so high, he could've been a small girl. From the rest of the conversation, I infer that the nurses interfered with his beeline. The nurse with the gold necklaces stomped out to get disinfectant and clean towels. She didn't look at me.

When they finally got him settled back into the bed, he was breathing heavily, staring at the wall.

"Go home, Robin," he said. "You've seen enough."

"Can I get you anything?" I ask. I've already brought his dentures, wrapped in a washcloth, and a clean pair of pants.

"No. Go home," he said. So I did.

But now he's back in his small apartment, dressed in a flannel shirt and old-man cardigan.

"Have you eaten anything?" I ask.

"I won't go down to the dining hall!" he yelps. "They're trying to poison me! All those sauces. You'd never believe it, all these nonagenarians eating all that *sauce*." I go into the adjoining kitchen. Vegetable soup, ramen, cup-o-noodles, a stale challah bread, and Trader Joe's milk chocolate almonds.

"Can I make you some soup?" I ask.

"Yes," he says. "Camas." He's looking at her as if she just popped out of the seat cushion. "Where are you in New York now?"

"Park Slope," she says.

"OH," he cries. With that word his face expands and his eyes get very round. Then, as if pricked by a pin, his entire face collapses into a lipless grimace. "Such affluence!" he says. "How are the blacks doing?"

"The blacks?" Camas says, looking to me for help. I shrug.

"All that Crown Heights business," he says. "All that anti-Semitism! Such trouble!"

"The blacks are fine," she says.

The bottom of my grandfather's little blue saucepan begins to smoke. I lift it. Though the pot's not new, it still has its label, burned now to a shimmery crisp.

"The label's still on the pot," I say to myself, but Camas hears me through the open space over the sink. She raises her eyebrows at me and I can tell she's going to laugh and I am going to laugh, and once the two of us get going we won't be able to stop.

No order. Again I'm struck by this. After each event it is as if nothing happens. There's nothing inside of each everything. I am still trying to knit Don a birthday scarf. I imagine that my mom will die on his birthday and then I will be a bad girlfriend every year, mourning when Don will want cakes and presents—when he should have those things. I've switched from the brown-and-white wool to a fuzzy blue wool but this time it's too tight; the ridges make the whole scarf look like a big, thick thing you'd place by a door in case of a fire.

My aunt and uncle arrive, reluctant, from Long Island. My aunt fidgets over pots of canned tomatoes. She laughs nervously almost all the time, her eyes worried and sad. My uncle wears a poignant look on his face. He sits in a wooden chair by the kitchen window and gazes at the trees. My aunt makes spaghetti and meatballs. Spaghetti and chicken parmesan. Lasagna. My uncle's black hair hangs shaggy across his brow.

My uncle and my mother were never close. My mother got straight As and spoke in a musical, articulate way. She traveled to Europe. She studied art history,

French, Chaucer, law. She married a doctor. My uncle hung out with kids my grandparents didn't like. He married a Catholic. The older generations shook their heads, heartbroken at the idea of babies lost to white gowns and wafers.

All my life I've wished for a sibling. If I had a sibling, I wouldn't be alone under the suffocating weight of all this. I'd have relief. But as Dad, Martha, Suz, and I attend to the crust accumulating on Mom's face, change the bandages on her oozing sores, as we help her from the bed to the commode to the wheelchair, my uncle stares at the trees as if he's struck by the transient nature of life.

Over the summer, my aunt came for a week so my father could go hiking. She sat up late with my mother and me around the kitchen table, trying to bridge years of silence with gossip and stories. She filled our freezer with food, learned to help my mother with the oxygen. But her presence further underscored my uncle's absence. Even though my mother was clearly fading, he stayed in Long Island to work at the local golf course.

I don't know what severed the ties between my uncle and my mother. Maybe there was never a tie to sever. "I used to keep him up all night telling him stories," she's told me. As children, they shared a bedroom in the house in Brooklyn, a cheap partition separating their beds. "I must have driven him crazy." Or she might say, "By the time he was old enough to get to know, I'd moved out west and had you." Or she'd shrug her shoulders and say, "We just never had that much in common."

Whatever the story is, it's on its way out. When she goes, she'll take with her her memories, histories, trivia, recipes. And she'll take her version of this mystery, too.

♦ ♦ ♦

Martha, Suzanne, and Melinda have decided to get my mother a special chair, made for people who are no longer mobile. They've taken Martha's van down to the seedy part of town. All morning, Camas and I have been talking about doing something out of the house when they get back. We've been inside for what feels like days. But neither one of us can think of a single place to go. We could walk Mercy, but she's been up the mountain with my dad already. We could get a cup of coffee. But who wants coffee? Who wants to see anyone in the outside world? The outside world has gotten increasingly foreign. People smile for no reason, purchase sugary snacks, worry over leaky roofs out loud to strangers. Who needs this? No one in this house wants to talk about leaky roofs. We want to sit silently and be known. We want to be soothed by quiet warm hands. We want to be passive, have the world come to us. If we are going to use our tiny reserve of energy to strike up conversation with a stranger, well, it might as well be with God. No one else is useful. Not that God is being very useful—up there punching buttons on his death remote, smirking away.

Eventually, the women pull up. I can see them struggling with a mammoth blue chair.

Before she got sick, my mother was well. And she loved many things. Color, texture, light. She replaced the old gold carpets with wood floors, and these she covered with beautiful woven rugs. The sectional sofa she chose recently (despite the prognosis, to spite the prognosis!) took months to arrive and now it sits elegantly, upholstered in crimson so deep, it plays games with the eye. Her carefully chosen ceiling lights bend to feature the art—lithographs of Navajo women in bright colors kneeling over pots or lounging on colorful blankets under violet skies. On a stand in the sunken living room, a full-figured woman in traditional garb squats, frozen in earthy clay. My mom loves this piece. I've never liked it. The woman looks a little drugged, her unglazed eyelids half closed. I think my mom likes the abandon in her pose. The power and desire the woman embodies.

It's the way things fit together that amazes me, now that I'm on my own in a house that looks like an amalgam of hodgepodge. The chairs in my mom's life are all the right scale. The fabrics clash perfectly with the rugs. Even the books on her large built-in bookshelves look clean and classic—none of the creased paperbacks you'll find on mine.

The radiation my mom got during the second year of her illness damaged her diaphragm, making breathing difficult. Each year she could do less and less, and the house became more and more important. It needed to be the things her body was not. And now it is a gift to all of us. No matter how awful the day, we can sit on the sofa bathed in light from the giant windows. We can gaze at the patterns on her hand-painted plates, get lost in the fabrics of the woven pillows.

The front door swings open and hits the bookcases with a damaging crash. The chair is the size of a small

rhinoceros, upholstered in quilted blue chenille, a landscape of lumps and bumps with pink scattered into the
mix. And it has a skirt.

"Try it!" Martha says. She's still trying to fix this
problem, hopeful that it's just a matter of the chair. If we
can get Mom to sit in this chair, then she'll be able to
sleep sitting up and we won't have these nights anymore—these nights that never end. And after Mom
rests she'll start making sense again. Because you can't
blame the drugs for her jangled sentences. Any of us
would stop making sense if we couldn't lie down.

I sit in the chair and Martha claps her hands excit-
edly. She gets the remote that hangs from a crimped
white cord off the armrest. She presses it. Nothing happens.

"Do you have to turn it on?" someone asks. Someone switches the plug from one outlet to another. Nothing. And the three women look concerned. They've
just bought this hideous chair, no refunds, from a used
medical supply warehouse in the low-rent section of
town and they're *lawyers,* the three of them, and they
never get swindled.

"It does work," Martha says. "It worked in the
store."

Camas and I take this opportunity to sneak out the
front door. If my mom buzzes, plenty of people can
help her.

We sit at the large wooden table at the knitting
store, surrounded by colorful fibers and stacks of pretty
books. We listen to the hum of the fluorescents and the
women who come in and out, dinging the little bells on

the door handle, asking about patterns and needles for the Christmas presents they're starting. There's a woman here, Sandra, whom we adore. She's big-boned with thick hair on her cheeks and over her lip, and she usually wears a green, blue, and purple shawl that she spun and knit herself. She can fix any problem. You bring her your knots, your tangled stitches, your warped decreases, and she can undo them. She can knit backwards and forwards and fix holes and straighten twists. Camas has been crocheting all over the place. Her blanket is coming out in the shape of Florida. I watch my poised, beautiful friend focus on Sandra's hands.

Sandra undoes a few wonky rows and shows Camas how to make a decorative bump. Camas holds the yarn and tries it. She's very tense. She looks like she's sawing through hardwood.

When we go back into the house, they've fixed the chair.

"Sit, sit!" Martha says. I do and I'm slowly raised against my will up and then pushed forward until my feet touch the ground, and then some metal parts deep in the cushion start pressing my bottom forward into a stand. It's an awfully intimate experience to have with a chair. I shield my bottom with my hands as I walk away.

"Wow," I say.

It's dinnertime. Another pasta dish. I'll make pot stickers for my mom. But first, we need her to try the chair. We set the table. My dad goes to unmask her, to wheel her in for dinner. We cluster around.

An excitement builds. Is this it? Is this the answer we've all been waiting for? It's like we're at an unveiling.

Martha balls her fists. Suzanne stands very straight. Will this prevent the need for a nurse to come and sleep over? Will Mom finally be able to rest? Will this give her more strength? Will she then start to make sense again, turn this whole thing on its awful head, decide she has the strength and will to try another chemotherapy? And then finally, we'll get it right—find the one combination of chemicals that not only shrinks the tumor but annihilates it. We'll publish a book and sell a million copies: the necessity of faith, hope, will, and a lumpy blue chair!

My dad holds my mom's arms steady to help her up, but you can't grab her under the arms or by the torso because of the tumor mass and swelling. Martha and Suz stand behind her, spotting. Good God, my mom says, somewhere deep inside of her, where the real mom still lives, get that beast out of my beautiful house. It takes three people to steady her and get her perched on the edge of the chair. She heaves. Her whole body's absorbed in the action of trying to get enough air. Her swollen hands clamp the cushion tightly.

"Lean back," Melinda says. There's about a foot and a half of cushion behind my mom's rear, but she refuses to scoot back. To us, it's just a few inches. But to my mom's fragile diaphragm and toasted lungs, it's the distance to the moon. I put my hands on her shoulders, just to make sure. I press gently.

"Can you scoot back?" I ask. We all take turns asking.

"Just a few inches, Jack, you can do it, that's it, just a few inches, can you try it?"

"No," she says, and shakes her head.

And it's over, all our hope, just like that.

My mom and I have very different ways of remembering. She remembers my childhood as one long happy stretch of days and has a hard time telling me any specific memories. While I remember very little, the memories I have are clear.

I am ready to get out of the bath. I'm young enough that my mother lifts me out and puts a faded brown towel over my head, covering me almost entirely. I stand on the woolly bath mat with the towel hanging over me and I must think it's funny, I must be standing there on my reedy legs giggling, because she invents the game. She creeps back and forth in the bathroom, saying, "I think I need a wild mushroom for the salad. Where can I find a wild mushroom?" I hear her pick up the soap dish, fuss with the bowl of the cat's food by the sink. She opens a cabinet, rustles in the magazine basket. Then she stops in front of me and says, "Oh look! I found one!" She grabs me and swings me into her arms. "Yum!" she cries, whisking me down the hall toward the kitchen. "A big one! Now I'm going to chop it up for the salad!" She hums a little tune as she plunks me on the cutting board.

I squeal and scream, "No! No!"

"Let's see," she says. "What's the best way to do this . . ."

Finally, she lifts the towel and says, "This is no mushroom! It's Robin!" I look at the bowl of salad, the tomato wedges and cucumber circles. Every salad exactly the same. Then she scolds, "I was just about to chop you up!"

I once told Don about this and he didn't look amused. But my mother and I got the joke, understood inherently why it was funny.

I miss this mother. She is already gone.

Cher's been cleaning the house once a week for fourteen years. My mother did the legal work for her divorce. Then a few years later divorced her daughter, too. Cher's a tall, weathered, bottle-redhead with a husky smoker's voice. She's studying to be a phlebotomist, but until she's certified, she spends her nights caretaking for terminally ill patients. Now that my queenly mother—once so bossy—is a heap on the bed, Cher sees a chance to put her knowledge to use.

"I love y'all so much!" Cher repeats in a theatrical tone I'm having trouble reading, tears in her eyes. "I just do, I just do! Your poor mama." She wipes the counter-tops with soft rags and orders us into rooms, into hall-ways so she can mop. The smell of Lysol. The smell of my aunt's canned tomatoes in a pot. The smell of dogs and Oregon air, always a little metallic and piney. Cher listens to conservative talk radio, despite a houseful of intense left-wing lawyers. We stand in hallways and listen to angry men rail against homosexual marriage and abor-tion.

I walk into the bedroom to see how Mom's doing. While Cher washes her sheets, Mom lies under a blanket on the hospital bed. No matter how much we straighten this room, it still looks bad. Mismatched purple bedding tangles with dirty nightgowns in the corner. We've moved her beautiful handmade nightstands out, and in their place have crammed a table between the hospital bed and the real bed where the medications and the BiPAP machine sit, draped in tubing and bandages. We moved the television on top of the dresser. All sorts of other clutter has accumulated there, too. Baby wipes. More bandages. The pillbox. My mom's been sitting up, dazed and scared. She keeps saying, "It's so horrible here, I want to go home."

Cher comes in, gathers up a mess of tissues.

"Your mama's gonna become incontinent," she whispers. "You're gonna need to buy a waterproof mattress pad." Cher doesn't attempt to mask the thrill in her voice.

This news travels fast around the house. Everyone wants to be the one to get the mattress pad. We discuss with gravity where one might buy such a thing. Kmart has gone out of business. The department stores won't carry it. Ross is no guarantee. We can *do* this. We all love to do. The more we can do, the less we have to sit and stare at trees and think about the transient nature of life.

It happens to be Halloween. The pumpkin I bought one day to carve with my mother—when was this—is it possible this was only a couple of weeks ago?—still sits by the living room stairs. We have no candy, just half a bag of chocolates my aunt brought. And Camas wants more yarn and I need bigger knitting needles—I'm going to attempt this scarf for the third time.

Oh, the air through the car windows, stinging cold.

We've stuck Mercy in the back of the car and she sits staring at us with her worried dark eyes, perched with perfect posture as Camas and I careen down the hills, past the high school where we met thirteen years ago, past the bagel store where we used to eat daily, religiously, past the Dumpsters where the stoners smoked, down past the university campus where Camas earned her first degree, a left toward the road that leads out of town, toward the coast we lived on together the summer I was nineteen, the summer my mom got diagnosed with stage four metastatic breast cancer, the summer we lived in a silver trailer under a sky that seemed so big, so alienating already, even before we understood that life was temporary, just a blast of light—we go past where my first boyfriend lived in a school bus he'd converted— it had a deck and a lofted bedroom and a woodstove— God, how my parents hated that—down until there's nothing but gas stations and porno shops and topless bars and Chinese and doughnut joints and Salvation Armies. We drive until the businesses thin, until the grassland starts to weed its way out of civilization, and Wal-Mart looms before us.

It's a new store.

In the parking lot, some teenagers are eating Halloween candy from a bag. The large breasts of a fairy princess ooze from a leotard top. A skinny, pimply boy wears plastic fangs. His buddy's some sort of green man. A piece of kale. The color of money. Mr. Radioactiveman.

"Halloween," Camas remarks. We get out of the car and stand. The sky dumps air onto us. And for a moment we're overwhelmed. Air, air, the wild sky, the cool asphalt of the parking lot that stretches on and on, out into the green grass and brambles. Tiny little sparkles fleck the dark of the paved area. The yellow lines that designate where to park almost glow. Mercy presses her face against the car window, steaming it up.

Inside, light bombards us. From a loudspeaker, music and a calm man's voice. *November second is election day. Please exercise your right to vote.* More music. More calm man. We wander down the aisles, looking for knitting needles and yarn. Camas finds what she wants. I buy some giant plastic needles that look like little missiles. Not so little really. Just missiles. Blue and green.

We look for costumes.

"Let's dress up." Who says this? Could it really be me? Am I standing over the sale bin, rummaging through pieces of Viking outfits, wigs, green noses? Suddenly I want to be a witch. I have to be a witch! For God's sake there must be a witch hat in here, I think I say this. I rip through the little sale bin, throwing wigs off to the side, sequined capes. I have to find a witch hat. I have to! The cheap fabrics scratch against my fingers. I make it to the bottom, breathing strangely.

"There are probably more costumes in the Halloween section," Camas says. And I see more teenagers in face paint walking the great distance from one side of the store toward us.

They're out of witch hats. In fact, they're pretty well out of costumes. I fondle a pitchfork that Camas gets strangely excited about. We buy candy. We get lost in the pet food aisle. I keep taking brightly colored dog biscuits off the shelves, pretending to read what's in them. Then I put them back on other shelves, adding to the total mayhem of this store. Camas finds a Dracula outfit for Mercy, but I don't want to spend the $4.99. I put a Brussels sprout hat in our basket for the dog. It's cheap, less than a dollar. Something bad is happening in my heart.

Camas leads us to the bedding aisle. We find it quickly. A plastic sheet. It costs forty dollars. Even at Wal-Mart, death is spendy. Back in the car, we open the candy. We don't talk.

"You're sick," Melinda says as I cram Mercy's head into the sprout hat. Melinda raises border collies that work the farm. They never wear hats or sit on her lap while she pokes at a dumpling. The sprout hat doesn't really fit, but Mercy takes pride in being the center of attention. She wears the knitted green dog sweater that's been lying around various closets my whole life. It hangs off her, too big, and her leg keeps getting trapped inside it. Martha squeals girlishly.

"We need a camera!" she says. "Ohmigosh it's so cute! Let's go show Jackie!" We all parade into the bedroom. My mom is strapped to the mask, her head propped up with seven pillows.

"Look, Jack!" Martha says. "Mercy's a Brussels sprout!" My mom gives the dog a bewildered look, but it turns piercing. Then she looks up at me and smiles vaguely.

"Maybe we can think of a doggie cocktail with Brussels sprouts in it!" Martha sings.

"A Little Shot of Mercy," Suzanne says. "A Mercyrita, A Bloody Mercy—now there's a good one. With a Brussels sprout instead of a pickled bean."

The dog wiggles free of me and I drop her to the carpeted floor. Her legs buckle and she falls on her side, cranes her neck, and starts to chew vigorously on the sweater.

Camas has gone to Roseburg to see her parents. The moment she left, the house started going to hell. Last night I tried to open the sliding door that leads from the kitchen to the stairway and it fell off its tracks and hit the hanging light fixture, cracking the glass. We had to take the big glass bowl out and now it's just a wrought-iron circle with bulbs glaring nakedly down. The heat pump won't work. We're either hot or freezing. Mostly hot. The men came to fix it, charged a few hundred dollars, and nothing changed. The kitten has started peeing in corners. And now in the steamy, broken, pee-smelling midst of it, we are meeting with Barb.

We sit underneath the broken light fixture—Barb, my dad, me, and Mom. Mom leans forward in the wheelchair. You can tell by the way she's squinting that she's trying to absorb everything.

"How's your pain, Jackie?" Barb asks.

How are you? I imagine my mom asking her pain. Her pain, which she once described as little trumpets— a whole army of little legged trumpets—replies: *We're just fine, thanks.*

My mom nods.

"Are you comfortable?" she asks. My mom looks at my dad.

135

"Jackie, do you have any pain?" my dad asks, reaching over to touch her arm. What Barb doesn't know is that we've decided to stop the anxiety pills and both sleeping pills. We've also lowered the pain meds. We'll only medicate her if she asks. We've had enough fun in the middle of the night, Barb tucked beneath quilts at home, her Zen water clock set to ding at dawn.

My mom shrugs.

Barb's aware that she's slipped. A subtle change in alliances hovers in the air. Her chin tightens.

"On a scale of one to five, five being unbearable pain, where is your pain right now?" My mom looks dazed. She gazes at all of us and then smiles. It breaks my heart, the way she smiles. It seems to come from the core of her body, more radiant and blissful than any smile I've ever seen.

And then the smile drops off. "There's no pain," my mother says and shakes her head. Barb looks astonished.

"*No* pain?"

My mom shrugs. Barb pauses, makes a note in her file.

"Is she still on the morphine?" Barb asks.

"We're giving it to her when she asks for it," my dad answers.

"How many milligrams has she had today?" Barb asks.

"She hasn't asked for any," my dad says. A storm cloud passes through Barb's pupils.

"Jackie, are you comfortable?" Barb asks. My mom perks up.

"I want to be comfortable," she says.

"Do you want to be more comfortable?" Barb asks again.

"I do."

I know where this is going.

"You can take more medicine, Jackie, if you want."

"It will kill you, though," I say. My mom looks questioningly at me, then at my dad.

"If you take more medicine, you'll die faster," I try again. "That's what comfortable means." My mom looks at Barb. Then she looks to my father.

"The narcotics will speed the process," he says decisively.

Ha! He fills the room up, my usually stoic doctor dad. I feel giddy with it—the alliance. It's us against Barb, against cancer, tumors, bleakness, and death. We're not going gentle into that good night! And because of the degrees, the years of work that took him out of our house, away from my mom, away from me— we'll win this. Barb can't argue meds with a doctor.

"It's a decision, Jackie," she says. Barb's eyes are reptilian and cool, but she's smiling. "You can be more comfortable or you can try and be more alert."

"I want to be more alert," my mom says. I can feel her getting closer to me as she says this, as if she can throw her heat my way. There's want in her eyes now, also heartbreaking. She's lost all traces of wryness, of edge. The desire in her is the desire of infants.

Barb's mouth tightens. I imagine her black faux leather bag full of morphine bottles, full of fentanyl patches with no home. What will she do with it all?

"And I want to be more comfortable," my mom finishes.

Barb perks up.

"Well, Jackie," she says slowly, "I understand that. But both things aren't possible. You have to make a decision."

"I have made a decision," my mom says. "I want to be more present *and* I want to be more comfortable."

My father breaks into a grin and shakes his head.

We agree that we will wait. We will see. We are armed with dropper bottles and enough drugs to sail the ship. But we're not going to do it, not yet.

In letters to me at camp, at college, my mother noted the flowers blooming outside. If on vacation, she'd draw the waves lapping at the shore, a crudely drawn sailboat dangerously off-kilter. She used words like *sparkle, amazing, beautiful, captivating, sun-drenched, happy.* She went through prolific periods—sometimes writing me every week—and every single letter is a love letter, upbeat—determined to see the bright spots. And she laced them with detail—the stance of a dog on a walk, a snippet of overheard conversation in a chemo chair.

My father and I can never quite mimic her unfettered appreciation for things—or her blind fury, the flip side of the joy. We are the conflicted ones, the hand-wringers, the ones who pace around the house in the middle of the night. We are the brooders.

I don't know how she found the herons. The rookery is far from the house, on the other side of the river. Perhaps she went out walking with her friend (and extherapist) Joan. They'd grown close; my mother's honesty and bluntness—that intelligence beyond intellect that helped her win case after case—were so disarming. Joan decided that once in this life, you could mess with professional boundaries, and the two of them walked together on many river paths. Joan had fallen ill, too. They both needed oxygen tanks and so formed a two-gal club, giggling when bikers turned to stare.

My mother. I can see her now in her boiled wool jacket, zipped all the way up. Her black cotton walking pants faded to a dusty charcoal. Her feet, always so teeny, bound up in little green sneakers. Something caused her to look up into the trees—maybe she heard a noise, maybe a group of ornithologists were out for the day—and there they were, the herons and their awkward-looking babies.

The rookery became an obsession. My father jumped on board. "Let's go see the herons," he'd say, when my mother's spirits sank, when she grew depressed from too much time in the house. She struggled to find things she could do with my father. He loved to climb peaks and travel the world, eat oysters and see canyons, and she, with her paralyzed diaphragm and drug regimens could barely climb three steps. So this was the center of their Venn diagram, the place they could meet. My father would find her jacket, load the wheelchair into the hated Ford. He'd settle my mother into the front seat, securing her green oxygen canister in a backpack. They would return buoyant, proud of the birds, proud of themselves. They would return full of something, a kind of peace.

Robin Romm

But, the herons. I've gone out there, dragged my exhausted body to the base of those trees near the river. I've stood with my mother, craning my neck, the wet morning air pricking over my cheeks, dampening my hair and the insides of my ears. There they are, eating their heron food, pooping their heron poop. They look like big, handsome birds, to me. Just birds.

Maybe my upbringing spoiled me. Raised on the edge of wilderness, I biked and hiked, backpacked and paddled. Unlike my urban parents, raised hundreds of miles from bears and mountain lions, the natural world, for me, was simply part of the fabric of life. I found it pretty when orange and pink light spilled over the scummy water of Dexter Reservoir. I knew that wood ears grew from the trunks of trees and that you could dye wool with lichen you collected from branches. Certainly the aquamarine of a glacier's crevasse had the power to hush me, the smell of old ice, a kind of danger. I collected animal bones on wilderness trips—antlers, a marmot skull, a deer skull, and once, something big, maybe the leg of a bear. It's not that I am not moved by these things, that I don't want them in my life. But lately, their power has diminished.

I don't know why I can't let the birds in. I haven't wanted to go up Mount Pisgah with my father, haven't been able to find any solace in the movement of the river. I know that I need the proximity to mountains and trees—couldn't live in New York because it's just too far from the West, from the glaciers, from the herons. But these days, I want no part of it. I'd much rather be holed up with a ball of yarn, tucked inside the

The Mercy Papers

safety of the house with my mother. Out there, you must come to grips with the rot and bone, bloom and disintegration. It's part of the world, this ruthlessness, this severed leg, this sun-bleached skull. I can't really stand it. All the signs point toward change, and all that means is death.

"Do you want a milkshake?" my aunt asks. Her hair falls in loose curls. She has large, puffy lips. Her clothes are comfortable, faded. My mother will eat only four things: milkshakes, wonton soup, pot stickers, and Popsicles. Popsicles are getting more challenging because she can't really hold them still and when they fall to the ground they break. My mom sits on the bed, gripping the edge of the mattress fearfully, as if she floats high above earth, as if she's on a magic carpet and might fall if she loosens her grasp.

It looks as though we've been beating her. Lesions have opened all around her nose and forehead where the BiPAP mask sits. The other night, the mask broke and the oxygen company didn't have a backup mask and so for hours we sat trying to hold it to her face, scared we weren't giving her enough air to keep her alive, and finally my uncle—who comes from his hotel room for a couple of hours a day—taped it together with gauze tape. The mask hurts her where it sits over the lesions and she keeps crying to have us take it off. But she has a hard time getting enough air on the regular cannula. And anyway, she keeps ripping the cannula out of her nose, holding it away from her body as if it's a cluster of worms, and asking why she needs it.

141

My mother sits on the bed, opening and shutting her mouth, making strange babbling sounds.

"Sweetie, do you want some soup?" my aunt asks my mom through nervous giggles. "Sweetie?" She pats my mom in little staccato pats near her neck. My mom has a gleam in her eye. She's trying to tell us something. She makes writing gestures with an imaginary pen.

"A pen?" I ask. I scramble to the dresser, grab the day planner we use to keep track of the meds and an old ballpoint and hand this to my mom. We're all transfixed. She takes the pen and continues to talk in another language, babble speak. She's poised to write and she furrows her brow. Then she brings the pen down to the paper.

We wait; Mom drags the pen up and back, up and back. She appears to be drawing treelike things, but violently. Kathy, my aunt, suffers a new bout of giggles. Suz shoots her a deathly look.

"I'm not laughing at you, Jackie," my aunt says. "I'm laughing at myself."

"I'll go get her a milkshake," Martha says.

"Do you want a milkshake, Jack?" Suz asks.

"How ya doing sweetie?" my aunt asks. My mom whirs. I can see it under the surface.

"Do you want a milkshake?" my aunt asks.

"Do you want some soup, Jack?" Martha says, "Some wonton soup?"

"A milkshake?"

"Can we get you any food, sweetie?"

"Some soup or a milkshake?"

"Sweetie? How ya doing?"

"What about a milkshake?"

"Can we get you anything?"

"Sweetie?"

My mom finally leans back, turns her wide angry eyes on my aunt, who continues to tap my mom's shoulder with her palm, and says, "ENOUGH WITH THE PATTING." My aunt is giggling so hard now, she has to leave the room.

Later my dad comes in with a Coke. Her new mask works better and she and I sit, staring at the screen on the window.

"Do you want some Coke?" he asks. He doesn't wait for an answer. He sits next to her and thrusts the pink straw through the hole in her mask, jabbing her in the chin. She leans back with a start and helplessly tries to open her mouth. He jabs her again.

We've all gone crazy trying to get her to do stuff. Martha's been frantically trying to get Mom to look at the flowers outside. Suzanne wants her to listen to poetry. I want her to talk to me. My dad wants her to drink a Coke. My aunt wants to feed her things. Barb wants her to die. And we all say we're just doing what she wants.

When she's finally situated in the bed, my father has a panic about a doll in the glass cabinet. It's a Southwestern Storyteller doll and a long time ago, Cher knocked one of the babies off it. He has realized that my mother is the only person in the world that might know where the baby is. He opens and closes the drawers in the kitchen, gets on his hands and knees to paw through bags of paper napkins below the cabinets.

"I don't know how I'll ever find anything," he says.

"Maybe you should go in there and ask her where

she put it," Martha says. My father grimaces. Martha's suggestion strikes us all as absurd. Ask her? She can't even sign her name! But finally, flanked by Martha, Suzanne, and me, my father enters the bedroom. My mother has her eyes closed. The machine whirs. The room feels close and dark, crowded because of the hospital bed. He stands over her until she opens her eyes.

What? her eyes say. What is it *now*?

"Jackie," he says, "Do you know where you put the broken baby from the Storyteller doll?" My mother gestures to the mask and my father leans over to lift it.

"The bottom cabinet near the wineglasses," she says. Martha, Suzanne, my father, and I go running from the room, down the hall. My father crouches and opens the cabinet door. And there it is, where it has lived for years in a small glass dish. A little tan baby, egg-shaped with jet black lines instead of features. My father looks like he might cry, but instead, everyone talks at once, everyone laughs. She's so amazing! She can rally, she can STILL rally! This is the Jackie Romm we all know—the one who dispenses legal advice, knows what's showing at MoMA, cooks cornflake chicken while simultaneously doing laundry and balancing her checkbook, potty-trains the dog, corrects your grammar, counsels sparring couples, and remembers exactly where she put everything. We are not so close to the end, Barb. We still have her with us. You can take your boat and sink it.

♦ ♦ ♦

Camas has come back from her parents' house and my aunt and uncle are up from their motel. We have people to feed and no food. "Go pick up a pizza," Suzanne tells my uncle when he offers to go to the store. Something easy, frozen.

When he returns he sets the paper bag on the counter. Camas reaches in. She takes out the box, then looks at me stricken. I see her start to laugh, an amazed laugh. I walk over to her and glance down.

Why would my uncle go to the chain grocery store at the bottom of the hill to buy a pizza for a house full of people fending off death daily, look at all those boxes, all those brands in their red paper boxes and choose a *Tombstone* pizza?

At the beginning of the summer, my mother decided to landscape the yard. It had always been muddy, most of the grass drowned out by the winter rains. She was sad that she hadn't done this earlier. She loved flowers and was the first to notice when the crocuses bloomed each spring. She hired a woman named Anne to do the work, and quickly befriended her. They talked about their daughters and men and the angles of rocks. The work began in April and is almost complete. Outside the two large windows in the family room, you can now see boulders and ground cover and a large lawn made out of moss.

A few weeks ago, my dad got a $990 bill for the moss. "Jesus Christ," he said. "Jackie, do you know how much that moss cost?" My mother stood in the kitchen.

This was when she still stood—it seems like a miracle now, the fact of this. A true biped. A walking mother. She stood there, gripping the edge of the sink for a while, and she grew visibly tense.

"A thousand dollars!" he said. "For moss!"

My mother's eyebrows arched. "She went out to the forest and gathered that moss herself," my mother said. "Do you know why she did that? Do you?" The bill seemed to wilt in my father's hands. "Because she wanted to seed it and it would have taken two years to come up. Two years. And I told her I wouldn't be here in two years and I wanted to see it—" She started crying. The tubes got clogged and my mother's eyes gaped as she yanked them out. My father went to her but she pushed him away.

"And you have the nerve to care about it! It could cost ten thousand dollars and it would still be worth it! Why don't you understand?"

"I'm sorry, Jackie," he said. "I wasn't thinking. I'm sorry."

Later that afternoon, he sulked in the kitchen.

"It's still a lot for moss," he said.

I have refused to do night shifts with my mother. I can tell that everyone is trying hard not to judge me, but I know my limits, and I am already so far past them that a night alone on duty at this point, when nights and days have stopped meaning anything to my mother and she's frequently up most of every single hour of every single day, will ruin me. And it isn't for Martha and Suzanne to determine—what I can do, should do. They go home to quiet houses after their shifts are over. They rest in the arms of husbands and listen to music and cry over tea. I can't go anywhere. I've been trapped for days, weeks, years.

My dad can judge me. I'm used to that. My dad judges everyone. I know he thinks that me saying I will stay with her during the day, but not at night, is the most selfish thing he could ever imagine, but I don't care. And the reason I don't care is that for the nine years my mother was ill, he checked out. He didn't sit with her week after week in that little square room with its armchairs and small television sets, while they pushed red chemicals in through syringes. He worked like a lunatic, hour after hour, paycheck after paycheck, saving the lives of total strangers while leaving her to wrestle her demons alone. I tried, in the failing and selfish way that daughters try. I called her daily. I visited often. I'm sure I failed and continue to fail, but he's failed, too, for more years, with more proximity—and just because he's willing to sleep in his own bedroom with his wife now does not make him the hero.

Besides, I can only relax if I take drugs to go to bed. And even on the drugs I am racked with anxiety, as if I am being slowly electrocuted over the course of the night. My dreams are hot, red, and angry. I can't be responsible for the tricky switching of tubing, of transferring my mom from bed to wheelchair and back to bed. I would cut off my thumbs for my mother, she'd just have to request it. But I'm my grandfather's girl— I can't wipe her off after she's used the commode.

"We should hire a nurse." How long have I been

saying this? Months. But no one thinks my mom will like that.

"I can stay over," Martha says.

"I can trade off," Suzanne says.

"We can take on the nights," Martha says. My dad shakes his head. We've refused offers of help before. My father thinks that everyone is just pretending to want to help. They're after Brownie points. Or afterlife points. Everyone trying to get into heaven faster.

"Why would you want to do that?" my father asks.

But we agree to try it. Tonight I'll be on until ten. We've scheduled Martha from ten to seven. Dad will go climb his mountain at five and be back to relieve Martha. And we'll start over.

In the morning, the skin around Martha's eyes is finely wrinkled, her face gray as her hair.

"It was an incredible night," she says. "Jack was lucid." This is hard to believe. And there's a competitiveness brewing in the kitchen—who can make Mom lucid, who can spend the *most* quality time with Mom.

"It was so amazing," Martha says. "We got up at two and had wonton soup—and Jack said the funniest thing!"

"What?" I ask.

"She said, 'Who would have thought that Jackie Romm would spend her last days eating wonton soup and ice cream?' And then she looked at her soup and said, 'Well, if that's so I guess I should have some ice cream.' And then we got in bed and she talked to me."

"What did she say?" I ask.

Martha looks deep into her coffee cup, considering.

"She said that you and your dad aren't ready, and that you don't understand how fast it's happening."

And I'm filled with a deep spite for Martha, for her preoccupation with needing to be the confidante, for her vigor, for what I perceive to be a certain smugness in having spent this time with my mom—*my* mom, who is dying. Who is leaving this earth but before she goes, she's imparting fragments of wisdom that everyone seems hell-bent on receiving. As if my mom's a prophet. A conduit between worlds. As if mumbo jumbo about readiness and timing when coming from her addled, dying brain has a new intoxicating weight.

I'm standing in the dining room for no particular reason. Again, night has found this little cul-de-sac. I peer into this ceramic vase that looks like the exhumed skull of an alien. My mom must have bought it in the seventies. Dripping with olive and brown glaze, it's really, fabulously, ugly. A stained-glass piece hangs in one of the windows, spattering red and yellow circles on the table, and I just want to stand here in the dining room and let the cool floors touch my bare feet. I want the smell of the house—doggy and warm. I want the draft from the large windows. What I really want is to be able to travel through time. I would be younger; my mom would be healthy. We would be in her car, folk music playing. She would be annoying me by holding the notes too long, after the beat, just to hear her own voice. We'd be driving to the department store in the small town mall to buy a slip for a thrift store skirt that I insist on wearing with work boots. Or maybe we're headed to the grocery store to buy the lettuce, tomato, and cucumber for the nightly salad. She'd ask me questions about my friends, the car veering outside the yellow lines as she looked at me.

I've started playing a game with God. I say: You can take my life three years early if you give me back my mother, without any health problems, for one full day.

One full day, I repeat to God. That's nothing! That's *one* day and you get three of my years. I wait for a lightning bolt, a crash of thunder, a little glowing heart palpitating by my eye. Something.

Okay, I will give up one leg if you give me back my mom forever, even in a really compromised position.

I've gone through fingers and toes, legs, arms, and love. I have offered to strip myself of many beautiful things since that's what God seems to be after. But he refuses to take me up on my offers.

And then I feel guilty, because I know all these offers are made in vain. I know I cannot get my mom back healthy for a day. I haven't had a healthy mom since I was an angry nineteen-year-old who couldn't have cared less. My mom is sick, sick and dying, and no bargaining will change that. And it's in all the books, bargaining, which makes me embarrassed. Look at me grieving my textbook grief. The trades I offer God are safe, because they're impossible. I know in my heart that I won't have to lose a leg to keep her, because she cannot be kept. Is this because there is no God? We are just a mass of cells and our cells make our consciousness and when we die, our consciousness dies—all our memories and histories, the calculus we learned, the case law we studied, the way we loved roast beef and pickles. It's gone with our cells, gone gone gone.

But until it's gone, it's here. And when I get a moment alone with my mom, which rarely happens anymore, I feel her alive in her body. She's still my mother. I still find comfort in her while she sleeps. There is still a person in the world to whom I'm inextricably bound.

And then I overhear Suzanne and Martha talking.

"It's gotten too terrible," Suzanne says. Glasses clank on the table, tea or Scotch. "I just wish she would close her eyes and not wake up."

"I know," Martha answers. "At this point, it would be a blessing."

Why are they joining the boatbuilders? Why don't they understand the impossibility of a blessing? There is life with enormous suffering and the dark finality of death. After she dies, there will be hours and days and nights of missing her, of a pain that keeps us awake, gnawing at us. It will have no answer, no antidote. That will be our blessing.

A few hours later, someone thinks to check the mail. Suzanne opens a fancy-looking card addressed to The Romm Family. On white card stock we read: *The Delta Oaks Veterinary Team is so sorry for your loss.* We search for words—remarkable that the local vet's office is so on top of the tragedy over here. But we're appalled that they've jumped the gun. It takes us a minute to understand that the card has nothing to do with Mom. It's a card for the forgotten cat, Arthur.

♦ ♦ ♦

The following day, Joan takes me to lunch. After this, she'll fetch my aunt and uncle from their hotel and take them to the airport. My uncle is anxious to return to Long Island; he's seen what there is to see, he's said his good-byes. Over the summer I spent here, Joan took me out to the river with her little spaniel about once a week. We talked about dogs and birds, we talked about relationships. Sometimes we stared at the water. She's got a gentle face—the face, I imagine, of other people's grandmothers: pastel, velvety. We drive down the hill to a Thai restaurant, her spaniel lounging in a crate in her car. The low brown building clashes with the neon sign in front. Maps of Thailand decorate the walls. Ropes of beads dangle from doorways. Joan orders a pumpkin curry and I order the spiciest thing I can find. And we start to talk about my mother.

"Are you ever scared for your own health?" she asks. "Your own risk for breast cancer?" Joan is Buddhist, which means that she can sit so still after she asks a question that she almost disappears.

"I don't really think about it," I say. "I've been too busy to worry about myself. I'm young anyways." Joan doesn't move.

"If I got diagnosed with advanced breast cancer and I didn't have a child—or a novel in the works—or some real reason to live, I think I would commit suicide," I say. Joan moves in her skin, just a little, as if she's experienced a tiny jolt. Her eyebrows rise. I can see her trying to figure out how best to respond to this. She doesn't want to minimize my pain, but she doesn't like the sound of this, either.

"After seeing my mom suffer like this—all the suffocating and all the pain, I just couldn't go through it. I've been staring at dying since I was a teenager. I know what it means."

Joan opts not to say anything and for a while I eat my mediocre ground chicken. It feels good to shock people. It's the only power I have.

Trading nights with Mom has everyone feeling frail. We need to hire a nurse. Martha says she has a sister who runs an in-home care business and she'll get some advice. My father calls hospice and gets a list of providers. Martha dresses up in her work clothes, gets a brand-new legal pad and a ballpoint pen. She goes down the list and calls everyone.

"The man is supposed to be the best provider, but he doesn't work nights," Martha says. She's drawn little stars around his name. "Do you think Jack would hate having a man?"

"I don't see how it matters," I say.

What's the fear? That he'll see her in a sexual light? That he'll want to fondle that purple, shriveled breast? But then I remember when my mom took me to a spa for my twenty-third birthday. She signed us up for massages and then made me take the masseur, who did turn out to be a total sleazebag, fingering my mouth and toying with the elastic of my underwear.

"You better ask her, actually," I say to Martha.

But none of this is real. We interview nurses as if we're role-playing.

They begin to come up to the house in tiny cars or towering trucks. Tanned, with lots of makeup, they wear rayon suits and earrings made out of snail shells.

"How long have you been doing this kind of work?" Martha asks, her brow furrowed, her pen poised. She jots down notes. "Do you smoke?"

My father will not permit a smoker to work here. Cher has been grandfathered in, but that's where he draws the line.

"There's no way *that* one doesn't smoke," my dad says of the most promising woman. I couldn't tell, but twenty-nine years of being a heart doctor has given him a kind of smoke detector. It's in the timbre of their voices, in the wrinkles of their foreheads.

"What's the hardest hospice job you've ever had?" Martha asks. She crosses her long runner's legs. Her black high heels look expensive. Martha doesn't trust that these women can switch the tubing fast enough. They'll get confused, staring at the clear plastic, plugging up the wrong holes.

"Caring for dying babies," the woman answers. "I don't much like that kind of work, but I'll do what needs to be done."

The potential caregivers sneak peeks at the rooms as they walk past. I imagine that this house must be a lot nicer than the average dying person's house. On the way to the bedroom I stop and try to see the laundry room from an outsider's perspective. You can see the deck through the large window, below which sits an antique card catalog. From a small silver hook in the ceiling, my mother has hung a little fiberglass woman flying with a kite, her arms clasping the string, her back arched in a spasm of joy. At some point, my mother framed a painting. In bright colors, the word *courage* splashes over fibrous paper. I stare at it now, feeling numb and blank until the parade comes back through, pointing out the bathroom, and I'm just part of it all again.

My dad has come to the conclusion that we have to hire one individual and also employ one agency. Why? Because people are not reliable, not dependable, and we can't put all our eggs in one basket. All the caregivers want full-time work, but my father's eyes are wild with planning, with scheming, with beating the system. He places a $700 down payment with the agency and hires another caregiver on top of that. Then he realizes the flaw in his logic, panics and blames Martha.

The individual caregiver, Sharon, looks like a Dolly Parton impersonator. Martha and my father like her intensely, though she doesn't seem fundamentally different from the other seven people who've come up—except that she's got on enough mascara to paint a deck and wobbles under the burden of her enormous breasts. She has crossed the perfume barrier—there's something primal and comforting about the amount of sweet smell she brings into the room, as if she brings with her a lush, tropical jungle in which to hide.

Sharon may care for Mom, but who will care for me? I know it's selfish. Barb has been trying to sail my mom, but now it's me who's drifting—maybe it's the same sea but we're drifting in different directions and I can't figure out a way to attach myself to Mom any-more. It frightens me and I can't speak it to anyone because being cared for is no longer my place.

I call Don but he's tired of hearing about all this—the repetitive nature of tubes and swelling, Barb and nurses. He has his own stresses. He works at a nursing home to pay the bills and people keep dying. He's had it with death. Death, death, death. He sees it all day and then hears it all night. He's tired of having no girlfriend, tired of giving over his evenings to listen to my anger, my fear. He wants a girlfriend in her twenties who can go to the movies, who can hop up to Tahoe and hike around a lake, make him feel funny, witty, charming, young.

Who's supposed to take care of him?

And my father's anger flares continually. He says that I'm selfish for wanting to go to the park with Mercy, I'm selfish for needing to sleep at night. And inside I'm sure he's resentful of all of us who cannot save him, who can't save my mom. Who is going to take care of him?

Who's going to take care of us? We are like little birds gaping for food, squawking in our nest. Who is going to love us? We can't love each other, we've tried.

We are going to hire a nurse.

Upstairs, Camas sleeps on a blow-up mattress. The first night Sharon stays with Mom, Camas overhears the following conversation:

Mom: "Aren't you going to ask me how I am?"

Sharon: "Aren't I going to ask you how you are?"

Pause.

Pause.

Mom: "Guess not."

Camas tells me this when we wake up and we giggle and then we laugh and then we really laugh, great splitting belly laughs that don't belong in our lives.

I've gone out to the river with Mercy. The sky is bright blue with puffy white clouds and the river, a cold slate gray. Tall trees line the bank. On the other side of the trail a dilapidated silo tilts toward a meadow. I used to come to this arboretum all through high school. I'd climb up into the mossy trees, watch the leaves, and think about—what?—Jack Kerouac? Boys? What was it like to smell river and rock, to rest in my solitude and not know about death? Who was I then? Sixteen with a scowl and a lot of freckles, ripped jeans and a vintage plaid blazer. I didn't like my mother. She worked all the time, and when she wasn't working, we fought. She wasn't like my friend Margot's parents—hippies who'd moved into town off a commune when Margot was seven. They ate organic bread and made little gardens to surround statues of Buddha. And I didn't understand her marriage to my silent father. I didn't like my mom, but I loved the world. I'd run naked into this dark river water with my friends in the middle of the night, having snuck onto the property through the woods. We'd ignore the pain of the rocky bottom, too invincible for that. We'd leave each other in the tall trees, whisper and pant frightening things in the pitch moonless black, just to feel it—that thrill of fear in a world that hadn't sufficiently scared us yet.

Some young men are digging a garden by a bench. Mercy begins the wide swing of tail and rear. One of the men stoops to pet her.

"What a nice dog," he says. We chat for a moment. Sun, air, trees, hanging lichen. He wants to know what I think of the angle of the boulders they've placed around a plaque.

"They're kind of symmetrical," I say. Mercy aims to jump on them. She's wagging her entire body and I keep tightening her leash. Finally one of them reaches over to scratch her on her neck. She collapses in ecstasy. When he stops, she sits upright, as if to say she will wait for him for as long as it takes, she will be devoted and true all of her life. "Might be more interesting if you moved one rock up to the top or something," I say, leaning down to take over the petting. The men clearly wanted to hear something else. They start grunting and one moves a rock over a foot or two.

"I'm sure it's fine," I say, though it doesn't really look like much. No one will ever stop to consider the jagged gray rocks sitting amid the overgrown weeds. But suddenly it does seem fine. Fine in a way I can't explain. I wish I could package it up, the stupidly placed rocks, the dappled earth, the sound of the river, the thudding of Mercy's tail on the dirt path, the determination in the young men's eyes, the deep stains on their canvas pants. The smell of the warm grass, cold water, old wood, a fallen tree, mushrooms growing out of wood rot, even my own sweat. I want to take all this world and push it in through that front door, crack open the house. I would run the river right through the hallway, pour dirt over all that expensive furniture, and then I would take my mother by her swollen hands, and go tearing into the dark, cold water, howling.

It seems like I should have nostalgic thoughts about my mother, but the one memory that keeps recurring is a terrible morning when I was about fourteen. My mother was flipping out at one of the many vizslas we owned. She screamed at the dog, holding a rolled-up news-paper in her clenched fist. The dog cowered under the sofa table. My mom was dressed in a suit, her hair tightly curled, her made-up face distorted in anger. The dog had peed on the carpet again and my mother had finally had it.

"Bad dog!" she yelled, her voice musical with rage. You'd think the dog had killed Arthur, who sat imper-viously under his grow lamp, observing my mother's fit with cool cat remove. And then she thwacked the dog on the hindquarters until it scrambled into a corner, shivering.

That same morning, as I was getting ready to walk up to the bus stop, she cornered me by the linen closet.

"Are you wearing makeup?" she asked. I was, obvi-ously, wearing eyeliner and mascara that I'd swiped from her bathroom while she was carrying on with the dog. "Are you?" she demanded. I nodded.

"You know I told you not to!" And then I saw her hand go up, up, and I flinched as I readied myself—she had never hit me. But she froze, her hand stuck above her head. "Get out of here, Get!" she said. And I ran down the hall, out those red doors, down the wooden steps, down the hill to the bus stop, my clumpy lashes catching the breeze.

Why does this image come to mind when there are thousands and thousands of other images of my mother I could cultivate? The mother that cooked us dinner every night. The mother that praised my terrible adolescent poetry. The mother who challenged me to do better on tests, who marked up my reports with red pen, who pretended I was a mushroom, who stayed up late at night with me working on a family tree? Maybe it's the mystery—her anger. The secret life she had that didn't relate to me. In a rage, she failed to be my mother. She was just a crazy, overburdened attorney with a young daughter and a preoccupied husband and dogs that peed on the carpets she'd just gotten cleaned. Maybe I need these moments. Maybe my mind knows it must put some distance between my mother and me. Because sometimes, when I am in the room with her, I am certain that when she dies, I will die, too.

And her anger only got worse. When I started sleeping with my first boyfriend at seventeen, she called me brazen. She spit out the word, sitting in the hard kitchen chairs, a plate of unfinished dinner before her. Disdain landed in her eyes—the real metallic glint of it. It scared and thrilled me, that I could do this to her. I could torment her. I could make her scared.

Oh, Mom, how the tides have changed.

Mercy hides under the bed in my bedroom. I lie down on the carpet so I can look at her. "Hi," I say. She starts to thump her tail and looks at me sideways, hopeful. I stretch my arm out to rub her chest, the thick patch of fur beneath the neck that dogs find soothing, according to my book. She sighs and shuts her eyes. I think she knows something about what's going on, though of course I can't be sure. She often comes up here for respite. Sometimes the two of us lie on the white carpet and examine the light fixture. She stays right next to me, her belly exposed, legs akimbo. She lets me hold her paw and feel the soft skin in between her toes. The other day, while doing this, I noticed that only one light exists in this room, in an alcove near the closet. I'd never observed the tiny flower on the white glass of it. I'd also never considered how dim the room is, how I must have spent most of my adolescence fumbling around in the dark.

I scoot back from the dog, stand, and reach into my pocket.

"Come," I say, holding out a peanut butter biscuit. Mercy, still lodged under the bed, uses her front legs to push herself out, as if swimming the butterfly. She sits in a silly way, with one hip tucked under her. I tell her to lie down, spin, make eye contact, shake hands, come, and stay. Though I've only been to the class twice (when I told Sue my mother was dying and I really couldn't come to class anymore, she shook her bumpy red face and said under no circumstances did she give refunds), Mercy's getting the hang of certain tricks. If I point my fingers at her like a gun and say "Stick 'em up!" she jumps spastically into the air.

After I give her her biscuit, I sit with my legs apart and she flops down between them, her head on my thigh. I rub my nose in her fur, squeezing my eyes closed, breathing her in. I want to feel nothing but calm, I want to seep through her skin and synch my heart to hers, because in this moment she seems like the chariot that could transport me. But the dog hears Lily come upstairs—the clink of her tiny bell. Mercy sits up and lunges at the stairwell, growling. Lily jumps on the half-wall near the stairs, unflappable, and begins to groom her paws. I lie back on the rug alone, to stare at the light, that small white flower, and feel my heart slowly pump blood.

The newscasters squabble over the election results and Martha, Suzanne, Camas, my father, and I gather with my mother to watch. It's a close race and much hinges on Ohio. On and on the commentators go. The election swings one way and we're all relieved. Then it starts to swing the other way.

"Kerry has to win. Something has to go right," Suzanne says. She's been sinking. She needs one thing to go right, just one thing. And for a while, it looks hopeful. My mother wears a plush white bathrobe, a gift from her friend the judge. The judge stuck Kerry-Edwards pins all over it and though she's too rattled to speak, my mother looks cheerfully like a billboard. We go to bed certain that the next day will bring good news. A new day, a new president. Bad things can't keep happening. But in the morning, Kerry concedes the election.

Martha and I go into my mom's bedroom to help her with the nebulizer. To see if she needs anything. My mother has not been speaking. She's so out of it, so dazed. But she opens her eyes halfway.

"Who won?" The words sound funny, like there is foam in her mouth.

"Oh Jack," says Martha. She looks truly sorry, her arms crossed, hands wringing her elbows. Why can't we give her just one bit of good news? A new president would delight her. She might sit up in bed and smile. She might get worked up, start talking about the good of social services. We'll get out of this crazy war in Iraq and deal with health care.

"Bush won," I say. My mother says nothing. Then she shakes her head. For the rest of the day, she doesn't move.

She doesn't move the following day, either. Nor does she speak. She's not interested in eating. Camas and I read her some poetry, but she makes no move to show us she hears.

We cancel the night nurse. We decide that one of us should be in the room at all times. So we set up a card table and a Scrabble board at the foot of Mom's bed and Camas, my father, and I attempt to play a game. Ordinarily my father and I are fiercely competitive. He gets words like *tuxedo* and I get words like *octagon* and we play until our blood is boiling, until we are ready to kill each other. This time, though, we're inching along. Words like *bell, fall, pool, boat.* We don't finish the game. We are all outside ourselves watching ourselves play with little lettered tiles while death sharpens his blade. So we move the board to sit with the rest of the clutter on the dresser. It's Camas's last night here. In the morning, she needs to go back to New York.

"I wish I didn't have to go back," she says. "It seems like really bad timing." We both know what she means by this. She won't see my mother again and she won't get the closure of being here for the end. It's so close now. There's nothing to say. I want to read my mother fairy tales, something familiar and comforting and when I'm upstairs, I realize that I'm looking for the Brothers Grimm book with the morbid "Babes in the Woods" in it. It's a story I loved as a kid, a story my mom boycotted. In it, a boy and girl scatter bread crumbs to mark their path as they walk deep in the forest, not noticing that birds eat them as soon as they fall. Lost, the boy and girl lie down under the shade of a rust-colored tree. The last illustration shows the birds covering the dead children with leaves. I stop myself and we content ourselves with Mary Oliver and starfish.

In the morning, Mom hasn't moved and Camas looks exhausted and fretful when we take her to the airport.

◆ ◆ ◆

The first girl I ever knew with a dead mother was a babysitter I had when I was very young—Annie. Her feathered blond hair always looked clean and she kept a collection of stuffed animals on her bed. She lived with her father in a large, dark wooden house hidden behind thick pine trees. I remember dropping her off one evening. My mother and I were driving through more trees to get back down the hills, to the road that led through different trees, to a different hill, our hill.

Though I saw roads and trees like these daily for years and years, in my memory the road from Annie's house is as dark and shadowy as the path to a witch's lair. The mailboxes stood pewter and cold. The trees towered hundreds of feet in the air.

"Why doesn't Annie have a mom?" I asked. My mom told me that she was dead. I considered this. I was five or six and this was a big feeling. It was like the word *war,* which I used to say to myself before falling asleep. I'd try to imagine *war war war* and what it meant for an entire country to be demolished. I'd creep up the edge of it—the idea of infinity and death—and then I'd shrink back under my orange covers, the cross-stitched lion roaring over my bed, bug carcasses creating comforting dirt in the light fixtures. Sometimes I'd shut my eyes and try to feel ghosts.

"How did she die?" I wanted to know.

"She committed suicide. She killed herself. It's very sad." She must have told me how, because I know that Annie's mother died from carbon monoxide poisoning, in her car, in the garage. I don't know why my mother told me this. Maybe she wanted to prevent me from asking Annie about it. Maybe it just slipped out. From that day forward, Annie ceased to be human. She was made of mystery and tragedy, porcelain and smoke. Off-limits, and a little bit scary.

At fourteen, I went away to a summer camp on an island off the coast of Washington. We lived in tepees and learned tribal lore. Once we camped near a haunted meadow where a legendary battle took place between warring native tribes. The winning tribe severed all the heads of the losing tribe and buried the headless bodies in the field. Their souls wandered the meadow and would forever, howling, looking for their missing heads. Katie Lyman lived in my tepee. She was a quiet girl with long yellow hair and sad green eyes. She was a year younger than I. Though she moved awkwardly, she had a quiet steeliness and no one teased her. She wore a lot of blue.

One night we were lying on our cots. Puget Sound lapped the rocks, wind brushed through the tall grass of the meadow. I held on to the wooden pole of the tepee, making deep marks with my thumbnail, and Katie listened to me tell a story.

"You remind me of my mother," she said quietly. Her mother was dead. It was just her and her dad now, in Seattle.

"What is it about me that reminds you of her?"

"I don't know, maybe your voice." She had me say certain words until her eyes grew frightened.

We stayed in touch for about a year, but then I lost track of her.

That same year I met Sylvie Anglin, a counselor at the camp. I fell instantly in love with her and tried to emulate her every move. She played the harmonica as she tromped down the dirt paths, dishwater blond ringlets swinging. Home to her was Mississippi and she talked with a lilt I'd never heard before. One night, as she watched our bunk, all the girls decided to play the one minute of death game. To play, you had to hold your breath and let the ringleader, Kaui, knock the wind out of you. Then you passed out and saw visions. At that point, Kaui led you back to life. Because I didn't care what the girls thought of me (I was already part of the little clique that ran the sneak-outs and social order), I opted out. I never liked people squeezing me or manhandling my back. Sylvie sat reading. I hunched in my sleeping bag, knitting a colorful and mismatched pair of socks. Sylvie's mother was dead. Everyone knew this. And now her father was dying, too. By the end of the summer she would be an orphan. The same smoke that made up Annie made up Sylvie. But no porcelain. She was too tough for that.

"You've got an old soul," she told me that night as she cleaned her harmonica. "You're going to do good things." The moon sent silver all over the dirt of our campsite. Far away, Puget Sound made water noises.

Who knows why she said it. She dropped all sorts of proclamations between harmonica riffs. It was part of her unpolished, particular boyish charm. She left camp early to be with her father and wrote me one postcard that I still have. It's of Elvis's grave and it says: *Hi Robin, thanks for the letter. I'm in Mississippi (see postcard) and struggling with my father's estate.*

Tara Bloom and I became friends our freshman year of high school at about the time I was trying to be a flower child, to get in on the crazy fun I'd missed by being born when it was all winding down. I wore thick socks with Birkenstocks and long flowing skirts. Tara lived in a small shingled hippie house up in the hills with her father, Amen, and her sister, Crystal. A goldfish pond glittered under a little wooden footbridge. Thick pine trees surrounded the property and a large

organic garden stretched out into the woods. Tara
taught me how to make elaborately woven beaded
necklaces. I must have gotten passionately interested in
beading one day, because Tara took me down to the
storage shed and rummaged in a box for a while. She
extracted a bead loom and two hand-embroidered hal-
ter tops.

"These were my mom's," she said, handing the
goods over to me.

"You shouldn't give them to me," I said.

"No, I want you to have them," she said. "You'll use
them. My boobs are too big for the shirts, anyway." Tara
had eyes like tropical seawater, so clear and green. You
could see little dots of tan and brown if you stared into
them. She had a way of being fragile and sturdy at
once—making you want to protect her forever but feeling, at the same time, that she might be protecting you.
I knew the shirts were special. And I always assumed
she'd ask for them back someday, though I wore them
all the time, for years—staining them at outdoor con-
certs and fairs. I wore that shirt through my first pas-
sionate love affair with the boy in the bus. It has been
fourteen years since she gave me the shirts—and Tara—
if you're out there, I still have them.

When my mom got diagnosed, four years later, Tara
told me more about her mom's death. They were hippies. She didn't have chemotherapy until too late. They'd
tried herbal remedies and invited a spiritual healer who
stood at the bedside while her mother died. I imagined
them in that house, the unstained wood walls, the velvet
blankets, views of wildflowers and evergreens. I imag-

ined Tara's mother to be as beautiful as Tara, that she closed her own green eyes and sailed out to death gently, peacefully, in the way I imagined that real artists and hippies would. Tara may have warned me that it was awful. She may have shaken her head and looked at her feet, but I couldn't see any horror in it yet.

"All I did was touch her arm and she started to scream," Suzanne says. It's a horrible dream, this. This. Mom's wilted on the bed, heaped on her side in a black nightgown and she's screaming. After a while it's like a song. It's rich with cadence, with violence and pain and a primal rhythm. It envelopes us, medicates us. We drift into the noise and can't get out of it.

"Are you in pain, Mom?" She's looking through me. Her mouth is open but oblong. My mother has perfect teeth, so white, so square and healthy. And a very pretty feminine mouth.

"Mom." I want to her to look at me. It seems to me to be the difference between this and something darker. Between death and life, life and dying, death and dying, hell and heaven, God and godlessness, I don't know.

"Are you in pain?" She continues to moan. Aaaaaaa. Aaaaaa. I take her hands in mine.

"Mom, Mom." Terror feels like a blanket. It's sedating. The whole scene is slow, underwater. We are measured and serene. "Squeeze my hand if you're in pain." She does as I say. She squeezes my hands.

My dad and I look at each other. He brings me the fentanyl patches. I take the paper square and rip it open. The clear patches look innocuous, but this will kill her.

Overwhelm her liver, which has been eaten away to dark lace. I press the patch to her chest, where it's swollen up with tumor. I have freckles on my chest, too. I smooth the patch down and go for the morphine bottle.

"It's okay, Mom. We'll help you." I take the dropper and she lifts her tongue for me. One squirt.

Mom. Mom. I want her to come back to me, through her eyes, through her body. My father lies on the hospital bed. We've canceled the nurse again tonight, it's too bad a night. Darkness crept up on us. The wailing began around dinner and now it's dusk and we had all forgotten that we'd called the rabbi to come.

She quiets when he walks in the bedroom. He contains all the sorrow of the world in his light brown eyes. We sit around her—my dad, Martha, Suz, and I. The rabbi asks if she wants him to sing the Sh'ma. She rocks her body in a yes. He opens his prayer book. He has a beautiful voice, like soaring.

The words drift around the room, old words. And it might seem over-the-top or comical if my mom were not wailing along with the words, her body spasming, jerking.

Mom, Mom, don't go.

We are walking down a gravel road, a late summer day on the Oregon coast. The weather is crisp but clear. Well, we're not really walking. I'm walking. She sits in her black wheelchair, wearing the daisy chain I made her as a crown. The tide is coming in. All afternoon, we've been fighting about a story I wrote in which I portrayed her as disabled. She doesn't want to be immortalized this way, she says. And I cry. She cries, too, and her runny nose interferes with the tubing. I hand her a Kleenex.

"If you die, and we're wrong, and you can come back to me, will you?" I ask. And she says yes, yes, absolutely, in any way that she can, and we hold hands and the sky is looming despite its brightness, the world is cruel despite its beauty and love, love is an awful thing.

Was there a road we should have wheeled down, Mom? Was there a turn we missed? If we'd gone upriver instead of downshore, would we have found the mushroom, the fern, the magic bean? The thing that would have saved you?

Suzanne and I eat wonton soup in the kitchen.

"When's Nurse Ratched coming?" Suzanne asks. I haven't called Barb and don't plan to. Mom is sleeping. My thoughts are stuck in a dark gray place. The soup is salty and the wontons are oversoaked. The skins fall off the little meatballs and float listlessly around the broth.

I take my Xanax, little blue pills, tiny warriors with the job of fending off an entire army of fear. I slink up to the bedroom, cover my head with the stiff blankets. I'm skimming a drugged sleep when my dad knocks on the door. I don't say anything. I don't want to know. He cracks it open. I sit up and wrinkle my nose at him, to show him I'm tired.

"Mom's gone," he says.

Mom's gone. I nod. My body is alert but I can't think. There must be a procedure for this. I peel off the covers and straighten my nightgown.

"How?" I ask.

"Her oxygen cord got disconnected," he says. "I

don't know what happened. It might have been me. Or maybe Lily. But I didn't hear anything." He grimaces and shakes his head. "Usually she would have screamed."

I wait for this to sink in and feel the moment, that moment in the bedroom become a permanent fixture in my mind. We look at each other.

Part Two

♦   ♦   ♦

They come in the middle of the night, the men dressed in black polyester suits with white collared shirts, their hair wet with grease so that you can see the lines from their combs. To me they are identical, faceless. If I close my eyes, the image of them dissolves. If I open them, there they are again with their remarkable facelessness. They have clipboards and lots of forms. My father and I sit at the dining room table. He tells them his insurance policy number in his low, serious voice, the voice that transmits numbers and absolute fact.

One of the faceless undertakers says, "Do you want to see her one last time?" His face crinkles. He seems to be smiling, though he does something with his forehead, puckering it in an approximation of sympathy. His friend reveals a great yellow shelf of teeth. Why do they look like they're joking?

I stand in her doorway. She slumps on the bed in her pink nightshirt, her face waxy, her eyes closed. I feel myself leave myself, as if I could escape the way she did, slip up the cream-colored walls, touch the crack near the ceiling that seems especially dramatic tonight. I can't bring myself to touch her, to get any closer, and soon the men are behind me with the gurney.

Mercy jumps around, excited to see them. Her ears stick up, bent over at the tips, and she trips one of them, tangling herself between his legs, exposing her belly. Someone grabs her and takes her away.

I have nowhere to go. I walk the halls of the house, looking for the place that will offer comfort. There are walls and glass cabinet doors and a metal sculpture hanging against wood. And I am standing at the red doors as the men begin to try to fit the gurney through with my mother on it. My mother who is covered by a black bag up to her chin.

They can't do it.

"Just a second," my father says. My father squats and fumbles with the old latch on the double door. It swings open and the night falls into the foyer—dark and cold. The dead fuchsia hangs, a black mass against the blacker night, and the small lights of the neighbor's garden walkway shimmer. They hoist the gurney up again but one of them buckles under her weight. I watch him shoot the other undertaker a mocking look. They are privately making fun of her and I stand there dumbly, watching them balance her, watching them tilt the gurney down the steps.

My friends pick up their phones, sleepy, alarmed. "She's dead," I say. And each time I say it, I wait for them to tell me I'm crazy, I'm wrong, I am not in Oregon, not in the dusty loft of my childhood home, holding a spatter-painted phone while Mercy whimpers behind the door. But no one says that. Instead, they want to know what they should do. "I'm coming," Don says. "I'll be there as soon as I can."

The sun stays behind the white of the sky the next day. I pour cream into my coffee and don't stir, watching it sink. My father hovers by the kitchen counter, his shoulders drooped.

"You made arrangements with England's?" I ask. "The one on Eighteenth Street?"

England's funeral home butts up against a parking lot that overlooks the Amazon slough, a greenish, brackish worm of water that harbors fast-food wrappers, strands of vibrant slime, and an occasional shopping cart from the Safeway on the corner. Kids from the high school a block away used to smoke there, on top of the Dumpsters. The brown building has *England's* written in dirty gothic lettering.

"The appointment is at one," he says. "I think you should come. Are you coming?"

What made the faceless men's hair so stiff? I think of the way they crouched as they balanced my mother. I think of my mother screaming, the feel of her soft skin when I said *Squeeze my hand if you're in pain*. I look at my hands now. I can't make sense of them. They look like branches cast in white.

I'm not supposed to be wearing this ring. My mother, months ago, had me take it from the safe-deposit box so I would know its history. My great-grandfather Jack used to wear it in its former life as a tie tack. Jack, the one who traipsed across the world in search of feathers. I'd asked her if I could wear it and she had said no and now, here it is, on my finger.

"I don't think I can do it," I say. The diamond spits a blue dot onto the wall.

"You can do it," he says.

A stocky middle-aged woman shows us into a conference room. The walls look like cardboard and the veneer peels from the table. A woman dressed in a red suit waits for us, her heavy silver jewelry catching the light of the gridded fluorescents. She takes the seat next to me. Her hair—brown, shiny, making patterns like wind makes on sand—is the color and texture of my mother's. She introduces herself as a representative from the temple, there to make sure everything goes properly.

A man walks in, beads of moisture on his fleshy nose. When he leans over to shake my hand, I see sweat stains blooming from his armpits.

"Bob here, pleasure to meet you," he says. He looks down at a form he's carried in. It's wrinkled where he's clasped it. "*Doctor* Romm," he says, and if this were a movie, which it nearly is, little dollar signs would flash in his pupils. His lips are too orange, like he wears lipstick, and they get wetter by the moment.

"Fifty-six your wife was, I see. I lost mine at sixty-two and I thought, too young. It's just too young, but fifty-six, that's a real tragedy. So you're a *doctor,* I see?" He smiles with his fleshy cheeks and hands us some brochures. I glance down. American flags dot the glossy advertisement for a funeral franchise. If you register online you can get special deals on funeral products as well as bereavement flight discounts.

I weigh in once or twice while my father talks, but mostly I stare at the wall.

In the middle of a discussion about how much a plain pine box is going to cost us—thousands, plus the cost of refrigerating Mom until she's ready—I interrupt.

"What are those for?" The wall plaques are all made of wood, though most of them have little emblems on them. The one that I can't look away from has a trout stuck to it. It's a rainbow trout, so it has green scales and a pink belly and it looks like it accidentally flipped from some glassy river onto a piece of wood and got stuck there.

"Some people, especially some Mexicans, like to have a photograph or inscription put on a plaque," Bob says. "Are you interested?"

I try to think of what my mother would say to this man if she were here. Mexicans? Trout? Does this guy have any working gears?

My mother, the Pisces, used to buy me jewelry in the shape of fish. And if she got to choose a vacation destination, it was always to Hawaii where she could snorkel. She painted streaks of color on white postcards for me, with the names of tropical fish in pen beneath them. *Put me on a fish plaque and I'll crack you on the noggin.* I do it in my head, despite her, stick the picture I found with a stack of old address books, on the shelves above the kitchen phone. She sits at her shiny rosewood desk, a coffee cup in her fist. A stack of legal work has been set before her and she looks young, vibrant, pretty—up to the task, ready to defend the defenseless. And there's the trout, flopped out next to her.

At this moment, he asks us if we would like to purchase a memory book to have at the funeral service. For only one hundred dollars the day will last forever and we can choose from a variety of covers.

"No!" I yell. My father presses his lips together until dents show in his chin. "We don't want to buy any of your *products*!" Why would we want souvenirs from this? It's not a bat mitzvah.

Somewhere in this conversation, it is explained to me that my mother waits in the room next to us. She's been sitting there the whole time. She wears a white shroud and this afternoon, women from the temple will come to perform the tahara, a ritual washing. The oily man nods, looking bored as the woman with my mother's hair explains what this means.

"It's a group of volunteers from the temple," she says. "They will come and wash her body, thank each part for all it did for her in this lifetime. It's very spiritual, a lovely gift for everyone." The idea of this makes me feel rigid, but curious. What will they see when they peel off that shroud? Will she look gray? Will her breast be black? Might she move one last time, might she twitch, might her ghost come oozing from her like in a film, white and transparent, made of light?

"Can I be part of the group?" I ask. My father taps a pen on the veneer table. He raises his eyebrows. The woman stammers and raises her eyebrows, too.

"It's not usually done, but if you felt you needed to

be there, special arrangements could be made." I see her looking to my father for help.

"You don't want to do that, Robin," he says. I look at him. He looks sad, patient, and for the first time in all of this, I think he might know more than I do.

I went inside the bowels of a funeral home once before. I was twenty-four, an investigator for the federal government, looking into a harassment case where the embalmer was accused of fondling corpses. I smelled the sweetness of rot and the chemical of embalming fluid for days after I left, finally shoving lemon juice up my nostrils to try to erase the scent.

If I don't go back there with these women, I will never see her again. I will never talk to her. I will never touch her. But if I go back there, lemon juice might not cut it. I might smell her death forever.

"You won't want to remember her that way," my father says. The patience in his face has turned a little bit desperate. *Please don't get weird,* he seems to be pleading.

And I realize that I cannot picture her alive—the only images I can conjure are the photographs that have become stuck in my brain, and the image of her still and cold, sideways on the mattress, dead. With the exception of her hair, which has landed on the red temple woman, she is gone and I am motherless. Everyone in the room is waiting for me.

"Okay," I say.

My father slides a credit card across the table.

"Thank you for your business," the man says. "I know Jewish funerals have to happen so fast, it's hard to organize them. But we have a great service online, there.

Good deals for people from out of town." He gestures to the brochure, which, like Barb's pamphlet, ought to be blank, but of course contains words, many words and numbers. "Be sure to check out our website."

As we leave the building and confront the day, I notice the American flags painted on the sides of the hearses, below them, the URL for the franchise. *Mom,* I think. *Mom.*

Don calls from Mount Shasta City, halfway to Eugene, and tells me he's with my roommate, Laura, and my friend, Kira. They've stopped at the food co-op. A few years ago Laura and I, on our way to Ashland, stopped there for snacks and bought mittens knitted in the shapes of animals. Laura bought brown lions with yarn manes and I bought yellow-and-black-striped tigers and we both wore them straight-faced to work and dinner. These are good friends. Friends who will leave on a moment's notice to be here with me, despite their busy lives—Laura buried under the chaos of architecture school and Kira with her time-sensitive fruit flies in the lab. I know I will need them in California when that is my world. But the thought of them at the co-op trying on mittens and opening organic smoothies makes me so tired. In some fundamental way, they're too late.

Everyone keeps asking, Are you going to talk at the service? Can you do it? *No I can't do it! How can I do it?* But I don't have a choice. Look at the American flag hearses and trout. Isn't it obvious that no one else will do a good enough job?

I sit upstairs in my bed with a notebook and I cannot picture her, I cannot make any words come. I thumb through the poetry book Camas and I were reading to her and look for inspiration. But I feel nothing in the center of my body but this whirring.

The next morning my father takes a look at the upstairs, the heap of blow-up beds and blankets outside my bedroom left by Suzanne and Camas, now waiting for Laura and Shayna, my New York friends who've cashed in miles to come. He says, "We need to get out of here." Laura, Kira, my dad, and I pile into Don's car.

The grass on the mountain has wintered to straw. Sol hunts down a wild turkey and roars after it, flying through the misty fields. Sophie galumphs after him and Mercy runs in frantic circles. We leave the trail, following my father through the boulders and grasses, rising higher and higher, all of us breathing hard. The sky drips silver clouds that cap the tops of the trees. Down below we can see the tiny town, so unreal, and orange rectangles—pumpkin patches still bursting with crop. Near the summit, my father finds the memorial, tucked away off the trail where few would be likely to see it. He's shown it to me before. Someone loved some-one and then they were bereft and they put this tiny piece of metal here and this means something to my father. He stares at the small plaque in its place among winter branches and brambles and my friends laugh at the way Mercy bounds, all four legs straight in the air.

Outside my bedroom, my New York friends are dress-ing for my mother's funeral. I hear Laura ask if she should wear the sweater or the jacket. In the bathroom, she puts on eyeliner. I have been standing in my bathrobe since waking. Standing here, standing there. "Are you ready?" Suzanne calls up.

I open the wooden doors to my closet. There sit the four green shirts I brought when I came here ready to stay four days. I have some jeans. The only other things I have were bought when I had to get out of the house, had to go somewhere. Once I went to a boutique down-town and bought a black silk skirt with tulips climbing up the fabric and a black turtleneck sweater. I'd liked the fit of the outfit and had no way to justify the expense. So I bought it, because nothing could be justified and it seemed nice to have an outfit hanging there. Something to remind me that there would be a future of dinners and plays and parties. I had never, obviously, had a chance to wear it.

Now it would be the outfit I wore to my mother's funeral. I would never be able to put that skirt on with-out remembering this moment, taking it off the red wooden hanger, clipping the tags. Don brought my black high heels. The heels are delicate, demure. They were expensive, too, bought years ago in New York for dates, for readings, not for this.

"You look so beautiful," Shayna says. Dark curls surround her solemn face. In college, in the crumbling co-op, we used to spend nights in her lofted bed, telling hyperbolic stories, outdoing each other. I look at her all dressed up, the way she holds her hands, as if she wishes, for my benefit, they were clutching a magic goblet. She keeps balling them up and then relaxing them. And I know if she could, she would give me anything. Anything I asked for. This summer she visited me here and we went to the cabin at the beach and found a black fly infestation and stayed up till midnight in our long night-gowns killing them with novels, one of us turning off the lights to confuse the flies and the other standing on rickety nightstands or the bathroom counter, slapping wildly at the ceiling.

For a moment, I am grateful for her. But I can't hold on to any feelings. I take the sheet I've typed, the sheet of words I will read up there on the bema. I couldn't do it, couldn't reduce my mother's life to a speech, so I did the thing they teach you in writing school. I gave myself an exercise. I used her red glasses, lying on the glass coffee table where she set them, one day, weeks ago, when she was still wearing glasses, when she still knew what there was in the world to see. I've written about having the glasses but not my mother. All of the objects that she surrounded herself with look different to me now, just as I knew they would. I see a wooden bookmark with a leather tassel, a box of museum note cards, a navy blue leather billfold, and they try to speak to me. Everything she has ever touched feels like it might have meaning.

I have been expecting this. In fact, I have been waiting for it. This morning I went into her closet and buried my face in the white terry cloth robe her friend the judge brought over, the one covered in Elect Kerry pins, red, white, and blue. It didn't smell like anything, so I went to the bathroom and grabbed her perfume and sprayed it all over. I knew about smell, the way it skips over your intellect, like the clicker with the amygdala, and indeed, it made me cry, though the tears felt jagged and unsatisfying.

"We have to go!" My father has appeared on the stairwell. My friends gather by the door. We don't have time to think about the white rose wrapped in paper with a card from Barb, left on the stairs. She's sorry for our loss and would like her CD back. There are cars and we get into them.

The synagogue is made of light brown brick, and near the ceiling, hippie-inspired stained glass catches the muted winter light. People hush. We are death's royalty. The rabbi gives us his famously sad look, his sympathy real but far away.

"There are so many people here," my father says. "Look." He gestures toward the door where a bunch of bodies clad in gray and black rummage through the yarmulke bin. He names them. My mother's teachers and deans from the law school, judges who listened to her arguments, community activists. And there's the woman from Colombia whose husband divorced her while she was out of the country, thereby trapping her in Latin America, keeping her baby with him in Oregon. My mother stayed late at work, researching treaties and international law in order to get her baby back. My father keeps turning his head to see who has shown up. I don't recognize many people. I see their suits, their stockings, the glint of their necklaces. My father ticks off names until the rabbi gets up there and clears his throat.

When it's my father's turn to speak, he walks slowly to the bema in his nicest suit and unfolds a piece of legal paper.

On it: all the things he will miss about my mother, the things that he could not tell her.

After the service, people approach my father to say that she's still with us, she heard all those wonderful things. I'd love to take my palm and press all of their noses flat. My father's chummy and cheery and slapping backs. I stand next to him, making the faces I think I am supposed to make. Sometimes I smile a faraway smile. Sometimes I make my eyes tragic or dull. As I gave my speech I noticed one of the Lauras tearing up in the audience. Instead of feeling closer to her, I felt a flicker of rage that she could be there, in the audience, as if this were a spectacle, as if this were a ceremony to be experienced. Don't they understand that my life has been irrevocably altered? That I am not the same person who packed her bag in Berkeley a few weeks ago? Will I ever belong in their world again? Their world where death happens to other people? I'm having so much trouble fighting off the closed cold of resentment. I don't want to be a window into the awesomeness of immortality. And right now I cannot imagine what else all these people are doing here.

My father continues to list the guests, though I don't recognize any of the names. "We should have gotten the memory book," my father says, shaking his head at me.

Because we're short on relatives out here in Oregon, the number of Jews we need for a minyan at the burial is lacking. My mother asked for a Jewish burial and so we wander around counting and recounting. The rabbi told us we don't need ten Jewish men, ten Jews will do.

One of my dad's friends rolls his eyes at the rabbi and says, "You don't need to be Jewish, if you've slept with a Jew you'll do." And for some reason, in the middle of everything, this strikes my dad as hilarious. Hilarious! If you've slept with a Jew you'll do! He keeps coming up to me, in between greeting people, saying that Don can count as an honorary Jew. Coming from my father, this makes my stomach lurch.

In order to get to the graves at the historic cemetery, you must hike through trees up a dirt path. Then, under the cover of fallen leaves, in the tangle of bushes, you start to see the stones. We slip a little in the mud. On the way up, a giant log-shaped tombstone towers in a muddy patch, reminding visitors of the history of this timber town. In high school, we came here during English class to meditate on Thoreau and write in our journals. I wrote about eternity in flowery prose, smelling the damp dirt, studying the patches of blue sky through the branches. Now we gather near the plot my mother chose, the fog softening the air.

We've asked a few random people to make the minyan and they mix with my father, grandfather, Martha, Suzanne, and my friends—two of whom (Shayna and Kira) count. There's a lot of whispering and excessive politeness as the guests step behind my father and me.

I don't feel the way I am supposed to feel. I don't feel grief. I feel irritation. My grandfather has been talking about my mother as if he is lecturing to a class of interested pupils. "She was too smart!" he yelped in the car, his voice cracking under the drama of it all. "Too smart for her own good!" I put one foot in front of the other on the way to the grave.

Through the trees I see bright colors—blue and green, hallucinogenic. On closer look, it appears that someone has put Astroturf down on the forest floor. On it, twelve folding chairs sit, covered in electric blue fur. Maybe students from the University are making an art film? We will stand in the woods and sing our sad songs to God, my grandfather yelping in Hebrew now, and they will have us in the background of their story, whatever it is. I crane my neck, looking for the camera.

And then I realize what's happening. We are stopping at the Astroturf. England's has done this. Has made nature into a surrealist stage. The smell of old cigarette smoke drowns out the wet earth and firs.

Heat shoots through me. A shady-looking man leans against a tree nearby, his legs stuck out in front of him, watching us with flat eyes. A cigarette dangles from his hand.

This is not how it is supposed to happen. I fly to the chairs and start ripping off the blue fur. Panic ripples through our procession.

"It's okay, it's okay," Suzanne says. The man from the tree has come over. I'm talking, though I'm not sure what I'm saying. Get these off here. Get this shit out of here. This is not a mini-golf course. The group starts to help me. We take the chairs away. We peel the Astroturf up. We can't remove all of it, since the dirt from the grave is piled on top of it, but we peel it back. The men from England's grimace and smirk. They tote away the electric blue and green. We settle, face the hole in the ground. The fur is piled behind us now. I can still smell the stink of it.

The rabbi turns his bearded chin to the trees as he sings. Old words mingle with the faraway sound of cars. The men stoop in their greasy jeans and crank the pulleys. We watch the box go down, down, until we cannot see it anymore. And, after a moment of silence I think might go on forever, sucking us all down into that hole, my grandfather yelps, "OH GOD!" and the rabbi takes up two shovels. He hands one to my father, one to me. We cram the metal into the clayey dirt and let it hit the box in pieces. A shovel makes the rounds. I watch my friends hold it. They act as though the shovel means something, like all of this means something, like it will mean something to me someday when I can tell them right now that it won't. This means nothing to me, this symbolic keening. This movement of dirt. I have no feeling, no ability to make meaning anymore. For so many years, my mother gave me meaning. I lived so she lived.

And their shoes. I can't take my eyes off their shoes. I know the stories behind them all. These shoes, like mine, have gone on dates. Have gone to parties. They are happy shoes, slingbacks and kitten heels. And my friends keep shoveling, getting mud on the soft leather. Everyone is getting mud on their soft leather, on the cuffs of expensive pants. Don tries to put his arm around me but I tense away. My father puts his hand on my back. I am tired of wordless touching. I want this to be over.

But it doesn't end. We shovel dirt and the shovel keeps coming. It's getting awkward. Suzanne takes the shovel. She looks insane. I feel a surge of connection. A sense of belonging. She is getting down and dirty with it, heaving massive shovelfuls into the grave. She's not okay. There's dirt in her hair, dirt on her dress. Martha takes another shovel and joins her.

I keep waiting, everyone keeps waiting for the rabbi to tell us to stop. But it goes on like this until all the dirt is off the Astroturf and the pine box is completely buried.

On our way back to the car, my father leans over. "What the hell was that about?" he whispers. "All that shoveling. Have you ever seen anything like that?" He grins at me. "Do you think I forgot to pay for something?"

Afterward, by the car, my father says he wants to see the herons. I don't want to go to the rookery. Everyone keeps trying to do the right thing. What right thing? Nature can't cover this like a balm. My father wants to go to waterfalls and Pisgah. He wants his dogs to bound through fields. He wants to see the baby herons and have them remind us that life is a cycle and that it will keep revolving and maybe someday darkness will turn to light, but I don't want this. I want to sit shiva the real way. I want to wear black and sit on a box and wail.

But I have no choice and for a while, I make my way among the leaves and mud. But it's November; the herons have long abandoned their nests. We stare at the empty trees.

We arrive at a house full of people in blazers and wool pants, eating bagels with tuna fish, bagels with lox. Fruit and cookies. Some we know and some have come from the temple, sent by the rabbi, who has had to go to a convention, to give us the illusion of community.

I wander back and forth, between rooms, watching people from my past parade through with waxy cups of iced tea. And then I see a woman with a heavy strand of pearls lean in to my father. She looks delighted by something, the powder on her face barely concealing a dampness on her brow. I pause to hear the source of her excitement. "When you're ready, Richard, I have this single friend, recently divorced. I'll leave you my number and you just give me a call." My father opens and closes his mouth, nodding slightly.

Upstairs, I try and get my breath back. I know I must want to cry, scream, plan the decapitation of the woman downstairs. And then I see what Mercy has done. Locked up here, all alone, with the knowledge that something bad brews below her, she has chewed a hole in the plaster wall. I kneel to inspect the damage and I no longer feel like crying. I feel like taking my dog in my arms and climbing through that hole, climbing out of this house, this small bedroom, down onto the little roof of the alcove, grabbing the branches of a nearby tree, swinging out into the cloudy sky, escaping.

Downstairs the party continues to rumble. The front door opens and shuts. Everywhere, the warm music of voices. And it's like I am in a ship traveling between worlds. Yes, there are people talking and laughing. Melinda and Suzanne look half-dead, moving from the kitchen out to the dining room and back. They'll wake up tomorrow and brush their teeth and make their coffee and call their friends or children. My friends will fold their jeans and put their hairbrushes in nice little traveling bags and journey back to what they find important. I am partly in that world. But I have one arm in another place, a place beyond the wall, through that portal. I can feel something creeping into the numbness. A largeness. A mystery.

I want to reach into that darkness and grab her back, grab that hand she held out to me when I asked her to squeeze if she felt pain. I want to sink to my knees and beg her to return. It seems remotely possible that she still could. And I feel certain that in a day, in two days, it will be too late. Only I can't sink to my knees. My legs won't bend. I can't say her name. I can only stand here, looking at the dog making her rounds, feeling uncertain that I will ever be able to live with the living again.

The congregation's other, younger rabbi, overly confident in his casual pants and plaid shirt, ushers people into the sunken living room. We sing the requisite songs and listen to people who didn't know my mother say what she sounded like. "What a lady!" My grandfather keeps starting stories and not finishing them, then screaming, "SHE WAS THE COMMANDER IN CHIEF! OF HER ONE-WOMAN ARMY!" Mercy sits here and there, waiting for pets, but as soon as a woman we've never met says, "Jackie must have been a real fighter! What a spirit!" Mercy races over and steals her bagel. I smile at the dog and shrug at the woman and people murmur all around me. Finally, everyone shuts up and we put on the slide show we've been preparing—Shayna, Kira, Laura, Laura, Don, and I.

The first images show my mother young, in a homemade satin dress, her hair ratted up, waiting to go to a party. Then she's holding a piece of cake on a fork in her high-necked, striped wedding gown (if you believe her, the only one she tried on). Sandwiched somewhere in the middle of the show she stands with her family in a Camp Kindering T-shirt and tiny shorts, one hand extended toward a canvas shoe. My grandfather and grandmother smile—it's visiting day—and my uncle scowls into the sun while grinding his tennis racket into the grass. But my mother is looking off to the side at something beyond the picture. For a moment, I get a glimpse of her then, her thin limbs fluid, some burrs in her sock making her walk funny. A friend gestures to her and she turns to look, smiling with vague expectation, her dimples hinting at their depth. She runs across the field to look at what the friend points to under the cabins, and my mother's heart beats fast from running and the blood goes into her cheeks and forehead and she has no idea whom she will marry or where she will live when she's all grown—she doesn't care about any of that—she wants to see what's under there!—she's giggling, breathing in the humid air, pushing her bangs out of her face, kneeing her friend out of the way, and she doesn't think about her blood, her breath. She doesn't think about the bigness of the sky.

No, she doesn't need to think about it.

How do I end a book about loss? Loss doesn't end. It goes on and on and on, written on every day that will follow. I probably should leave you with what Barb didn't leave me with: twelve blank pages. Here. Here they are.

Afterword

When my mother was dying, I found very few books that spoke of the particulars of loss. Much gets said about healing, but what of the violence of the actual event? It seemed to me that most books sought to close the wound, hurry it shut. But death doesn't heed commands. The wound, large as it is, can't close up in a week, in a year, in two years. You can't talk it away in groups, you can't meditate it out of you. The truth of loss is loud and ferocious. This book is a tribute to that truth.

My mother left me all of her journals. She began them in 1995, the year she got diagnosed, and kept notes throughout the nine years that followed. The diaries don't really create a story. They are moments in her world—the trials she argued, the clients she wished to help, the sun on the deck, a painfully detailed chronicle of the fights I had with my father. (Awful to read these; I can barely get through the pages.) Of course, there are days when she simply pleaded, but many days she wrote of the people in her life, the birds, the lazy dogs, new outfits, or necklaces, and her determination to see what would happen next, to squeeze out of each day a bit of joy, since she knew—though I could never quite admit it—that her joy had a limit on it.

She told me her plans for the journals about five months before she died. I'd come back to Oregon from Berkeley for that summer; I didn't want to live the rest of my life knowing I'd worked some dumb job while my mother whiled away her last days on earth. But the going was tough. I bought a ten-speed and enrolled in a ceramics course and every afternoon I went up to my childhood home, where my mother sat, zipped into a gray bathrobe. Every hour that passed felt fleeting. I felt I needed her to transmit information, tell me stories about my childhood. I bought a digital recorder and we tried interviews, though both of us felt self-con-scious and dumb, recounting, in stilted voices, our mem-ories over the kitchen table. And then, one day, she told me all the diaries in her study would be mine. I'd never considered what would become of these, and when she told me, the only thought I had was that I didn't want her to die. Which meant I didn't want the stupid books.

Months later, when she lay dying, she asked me if I wanted her to take out the parts that would upset me. I'd been writing fiction for years and sagely told her that she'd have no way of knowing which parts of her journals would upset me. She'd redact a few pages but I'd be upset by her description of the dog. She let that in, as she let in most of my decisions. She looked at me, doing the thing that always made me crazy—her eyes turning from openness to longing to desperation.

She started the journals for herself, before she real-ized she would die. But then, I think, she kept them so that I would still have her when she was gone. And I do, in a sense, though it's not—and will never be—satisfying.

♦ ♦ ♦

One day, while combing through this memoir, I hit a wall of despair. I turned to the journals, to this entry:

There came a moment in this journey when I freely realized that the lives most of us lead are small. Important, but small. Our radius reaches family, clients, friends for whom we do selfless and amazing feats. But our sphere of influence is local. . . . So our illnesses/deaths are small, too. Not unimportant. Just local in nature. . . .

Robin—I thought today how I would miss her so. Then I realized I won't miss her. I'll just be dead. And it seems so weird.

This was the moment I knew I would go forward with the book. Because she never imagined her death would touch anyone but those nearest to her. And I think, though she was vain and would have disliked being portrayed as sick, she would have wanted her journey to be something others could use. Perhaps her death is small, merely one death during a chaotic and violent time—but it is also large, with many arms, and changed the course of the world.

I am writing this note to you in a corner of a bedroom in an exceptionally small house in New Mexico. My life has changed dramatically. For so long, I was the child of a dying woman. It colored my life, it wove through all my writing. I couldn't move away from it because of deep loyalty and love. But now three years have passed, almost to the day. I published a book of stories, got a job teaching at a college, loaded up a truck and moved boyfriend, dog, and sofa out here to try a new life. Days go by now where I don't wake up to an image of my mother screaming, where I simply go to the grocery store, cut onions, and sing along to whatever CD has been sitting in the stereo. Then, a few days later, I will realize time has passed without her, and it feels wild.

I am reluctant to call this healing. I'm not sure I believe in healing. I believe that we live a million lives in our one life and that they bleed together, marble and muddy and melt. I believe that the girl who ran upstairs at nineteen to beg God not to take her mother still lives inside me, as does the young woman at twenty-eight who lost her plea. I am thirty-one as I write this. I am healthy, tan from all this new desert weather. I just walked my dog, Mercy, on a dusty horse trail and later, I will counsel students, who at eighteen, are just realizing the power of their loves and losses. Every once in a while, one of them comes in and tells me of a sick mother, brother, father—sure that I will not, cannot understand—that no one anywhere will ever understand—and the nineteen-year-old who lives in me falls out of me; my heart goes out to them in ways they can never imagine.

I did all the things a girl in Berkeley does after her mother dies. I went to a free support group at the local hospice center. I listened to women talk about the pain of losing their mothers at eighty, ninety, ninety-eight. I wrung my hands and kept very quiet, afraid that I would begrudge them their grief since they'd had so much time to be daughters.

I took walks. I drove long distances. I hated my father. I spent too much money.

I wrote stories and made readers flinch.

But nothing got rid of the loss.

If this book does land in the hands of those in the midst of a tragedy, I can tell you this: It will never leave you.

And I think in the complex way of truth, that that is the most comforting thing.

ACKNOWLEDGMENTS

It was the unflinching Nona Caspers who got me to start this book. Michelle Carter fanned the flames. Kira Poskanzer, Shayna Cohen, Camas Davis, Elizabeth Scarboro, and Suzanne Chanti gave wonderful feedback. Don Waters has remained my biggest fan (and love). And I'm so lucky to have the fearless, fabulous editor/agent team, Alexis Gargagliano and Maria Massie.

In the end, I owe the biggest and most complicated debt to my father. Thank you for understanding the need for this book. Thank you for supporting it. You keep proving the strength and elasticity of love.

The Mercy Papers: A Memoir of Three Weeks
BY ROBIN ROMM

Robin's mother, Jackie, was diagnosed with breast cancer the summer after her freshman year of college. For the past nine years, Jackie has been fighting to manage her disease, but the family believes she has entered its final stages and asks Robin to return home. In the ensuing three weeks Robin, her father, and their friends struggle to come to terms with the approaching loss of Jackie.

Robin Romm provides a savaging and emotionally honest exploration of the devastation she feels as she contemplates the eternal absence of her mother; there is no peace or relief from the pain. In her disavowal of platitudes about the passage of time and its powers to heal, Robin takes us to the dark abyss that haunts any of us who've loved and lost. Her wish that her mother's journey will be of some use to readers is secured as we leave this haunting and unapologetically forthright reality check on the enduring cost of loss.

DISCUSSION QUESTIONS

1. Robin provides an unwavering and unflinching portrait of her grief. Discuss the aspects of her portrayal that you found most compelling and/or difficult to take. What do you believe she risks in her revealing portrait? What do you think may be the value of that risk?
2. At the beginning of the book Robin writes about the hospice nurse Barb who is "building a boat to sail my mother out." Discuss how Robin uses the metaphor of boatbuilding throughout the memoir.
3. Explain the nature of Robin's relationship with Barb. What do their interactions reveal about the challenges and/or benefits of having a virtual stranger participate in the care of a loved one in the intimate confines of a family?
4. While most of the book takes place in the Romm's home there are several moving descriptions of the natural world. Discuss the sense of place in the book. Describe the Romm family's relationship to nature and the different ways the natural world surfaces in Robin's writing.

5. Compare and contrast Camas's and Don's reactions to Jackie's illness. Discuss their expectations of Robin as she managed her mother's illness. What do their reactions highlight about living with the daily specter of death? How do you imagine you might have reacted if you were in their position?

6. Robin writes that "women stop their lives; they're programmed that way" as she considers the number of women who come by to provide support to her family. In your experience, what differences have you noted between how men and women respond to illness and loss?

7. Robin exposes the complicated emotional minefield that springs up among Jackie's helpers (herself, her father, Martha, and Sue) as they struggled to make sense of Jackie's approaching death. Discuss their relationships with one another. What role did they strive to play in the household?

8. Barb suggests that Robin had the power to release her mother to death. Yet Robin believes that Jackie wanted "more life, at any cost." Describe Jackie. What were her strengths and weaknesses? What sense did you have of where she might have stood on this issue? Provide examples for your reasoning.

9. Robin writes that "my mother gave me meaning. I lived so she lived." What does this say about how daughters' lives may be informed by their mothers? To what degree does Jackie's illness transform Robin's life and how does Robin try to eke out her own space? How do you believe Jackie's death will continue to define or shape Robin's life?

10. Death often raises questions about the value and purpose of living. What lessons does *The Mercy Papers* offer readers about life? What will you take away from your reading of this memoir?

11. Why do you believe Robin entitled her book *The Mercy Papers*?

12. What incident inspires the book's cover? What do you think the cover reflects about the tale Robin sought to tell?

13. In the Afterword, Robin writes, "I'm not sure I believe in healing." What do you think she means? What vision of healing do you believe she is rejecting in this phrase? What does she offer instead?

ENHANCE YOUR BOOK CLUB

1. There are a number of resources to help individuals who have suffered the loss of a parent, particularly women who have lost their mothers. I've included a list of links below that also provide access to even more resources:
    a. http://www.connect.legacy.com/: LegacyConnect offers fellowship, wisdom, and support after a loss. Share your story, connect with others, find comfort and inspiration, and begin to heal.

b. http://motherlessdaug.meetup.com/: Allows users to search for support groups for girls and women who have lost their mothers, by zip code within the USA and by cities internationally.

c. http://www.momshalo.org/: Information and resources that evolved out of the website author's memorial to her mother.

d. http://www.hopeedelman.com/: Often referred to as the definitive book on mother loss, *Motherless Daughters: The Legacy of Loss* by Hope Edelman brought this phrase and recognition that early mother loss continues to affect girls and women throughout their lives into the public's consciousness. Her website allows users to find motherless daughter support groups, workshops, and events.

2. Elisabeth Kübler-Ross's 1969 book, *On Death and Dying,* offered us five stages of grief: denial, anger, bargaining, depression, and acceptance. With members of your book club, discuss examples of any or all of these stages in the book and in your own experiences.

3. Distribute the intriguing article found at http://www.grief.net/Articles/Myth%20of%20Stages.pdf, which challenges Kübler-Ross's stages. Discuss how *The Mercy Papers*'s unflinching portrait similarly suggests grief's uniqueness for each individual.

4. At the end of *The Mercy Papers*, Robin Romm leaves the reader with twelve empty pages to fill as s/he wishes. How did you fill these empty pages? Sample questions are below. I invite you to share your writings/drawings with your reading group members.

a. Identify a specific memory that continues to resonate about the person you have lost.

b. Give an account of something you do/did to commemorate or honor the person you have lost.

c. Provide examples of stories you or others continue to tell about the person you have lost.

d. Write a letter describing an event that you wish you could have shared with the person you have lost.

e. Create your own exercise.

5. If members are willing and able, invite them to discuss their personal experiences with death and dying. What elements within *The Mercy Papers* did they relate to? If they could have penned their own memoir of that time, what title would they have given it and why?

ABOUT THE AUTHOR

Robin Romm is also the author of the short story collection *The Mother Garden,* which was a finalist for the PEN USA prize. Born and raised in Eugene, Oregon, she currently lives in Las Cruces, New Mexico, where she teaches in the MFA program at New Mexico State University.

Printed in the United States
By Bookmasters